Practical Dog Breeding
and Genetics

Practical Dog Breeding and Genetics

ELEANOR FRANKLING
M.A. (CANTAB), L.R.C.P., M.R.C.S.

Revised by Trevor Turner
B Vet Med, MRCVS

POPULAR DOGS
London Melbourne Auckland Johannesburg

Popular Dogs Publishing Co. Ltd

An imprint of Century Hutchinson Ltd

Brookmount House, 62–65 Chandos Place,
Covent Garden, London WC2N 4NW

Century Hutchinson Australia (Pty) Ltd
PO Box 496, 16–22 Church Street, Hawthorn,
Melbourne, Victoria 3122

Century Hutchinson New Zealand Limited
191 Archers Road, PO Box 40–086, Glenfield, Auckland 10

Century Hutchinson South Africa (Pty) Ltd
PO Box 337, Bergvlei 2012, South Africa

First Published 1961
Revised edition 1965, 1969, 1974, 1975, 1978, 1981, 1987

Set in Baskerville by BookEns, Saffron Walden, Essex

Printed by and bound in Great Britain by
Anchor Brendon Ltd, Tiptree, Essex

British Library Cataloguing in Publication data

Frankling, Eleanor
　　Practical dog breeding and genetics.—
　　8th ed.
　　1. Dogs——Breeding
　　I. Title　II. Turner, Trevor
　　636.7'082　　SF427.2

ISBN 0 09 171540 7

(M) 636.708 2 F

CONTENTS

ILLUSTRATIONS

AUTHOR'S INTRODUCTION

The first version of this book, *The Practical Guide to Dog Breeding* (1953), brought from many parts of the world letters of appreciation of help in the practical management of breeding not readily to be found elsewhere.

This second version might almost be called a new book. It contains the same practical information, but the text has been carefully revised, rewritten, expanded where necessary and brought up to date in the various subjects on which our knowledge has been enlarged. We know more now about fading puppies, virus diseases and so on and the more recent expert views are included in these pages. The most popular features of the first edition, detailed management of mating, whelping and puppy rearing, are still here with some additions. Dog breeders are becoming increasingly interested in genetics, and owing to this a long new section on simple genetics has been added.

In writing the earlier book I tried to remember and make as clear as I could the points which had puzzled me as a complete novice. I have tried to do the same for the elementary genetics in this book. New words are perhaps the great difficulty of a new subject. If the reader will look them up in the glossary as they come along, and refresh his memory when necessary these words will soon become as familiar to him as the many doggy words which trip so easily from the tongue of the enthusiast, with the additional advantage that genetic words have an exact meaning.

Genetic principles are practical politics for dog breeders. Heredity itself is something more. It offers a glimpse of the mystery of life itself, its origin and continuity, its present, past and future. I should like to think that these chapters would stimulate the enquiring mind to discern these wider horizons.

E. F.

Bledlow 1960

Author's Note to Second Edition

The second edition of *Practical Dog Breeding and Genetics* gives opportunity for the inclusion of new information which recently acquired genetic knowlege has made available.

Newer remedies have succeeded the old in some directions, but these are the province of the veterinary surgeon. Fortunately Nature does not easily change her age-old methods of reproducing her species and the chapters on breeding and whelping remain unchanged.

Hereditary abnormalities have made headlines in the press and in some breeds they constitute a problem, the solution of which will depend, not only on genetic research which must inevitably be long and costly, but on the good sense and integrity of breeders and on their willingness to co-operate.

Defects caused by a number of genes acting in combination may be difficult or impossible to eliminate by genetic methods. Practical *ad hoc* means may have to be adopted for their control.

E. F.

Bledlow 1964

Author's Note to Third Edition

I must again express my pleasure to the many people who have found the previous editions of this book useful.

Few changes will be found in this third edition though one should be of interest to many people and we hope to find the solution to the problem it presents.

The fundamentals of genetics are established but much remains to be discovered concerning the chemistry of life itself. Let us hope that mankind acquires more wisdom before the day when these secrets are revealed.

E. F.

London 1969

REVISER'S NOTE TO SEVENTH EDITION

When the fourth edition was required the publishers asked Mrs Joan Woodyatt to revise this book as Dr Frankling's health did not allow her to do this work herself. Mrs Woodyatt further revised the text for the sixth edition, and I cannot do better than reproduce the following extract from her reviser's note to that edition: 'As a writer, Dr Frankling greatly enriched the knowledge of all serious dog owners with her books and articles, and her death in January 1975 was a great loss to the canine world. *Practical Dog Breeding and Genetics* in particular is used as a reference book by novices as well as by experienced breeders from all parts of the world.'

Unfortunately, Mrs Woodyatt could not undertake the additional revisions which, due to the passage of time, are now needed for the seventh edition, so I have been invited by the publishers to check through Dr Frankling's book, which I have known and admired for many years. It has of course been unnecessary for me to make any changes in the chapters relating to genetics, but some amendments have been made to the sections on round- and tapeworms. I have also rewritten the addendum on Vaccination and Duration of Immunity in the light of modern veterinary knowledge and current practice, in addition to making some revisions to the chapters on Puppy Management and Hazards of Puppyhood. The passages relating to Kennel Club procedures and registration systems have also been brought up to date again.

Mandeville Veterinary Hospital, 1980   T.T.

REVISER'S NOTE TO EIGHTH EDITION

In the six years since the publication of the seventh edition many new drugs and modes of treatment have been introduced and there has been considerable progress in the elucidation of many canine problems, not least those with a genetic or possible genetic basis such as PRA, hip dysplasia and certain forms of deafness. In addition certain Kennel Club regulations regarding breeding have been modified.

Careful revision has therefore been carried out in order to ensure that Dr Frankling's book can continue to serve as an authoritative text for all those interested in the subject.

In this edition, the section on genetics has been updated and re-written to include examples involving dogs rather than Mendel's original pea plants. In this way I have tried to make this difficult but important subject a little more intelligible.

Mandeville Veterinary Hospital, 1987   T.T.

1

Introducing the Subject

This book can begin with a few assumptions. First, the cult of the 'pedigree' dog is more firmly and securely based than ever before; second, the show dogs of this country are, in general, unsurpassed by those of any other country in the world; third, well-bred dogs are ever increasingly sold as pets to the general public; fourth, every breeder of show stock also breeds pets, and the proportion of the one to the other depends on the breeder's knowledge and skill, and, we must add, on his luck. In short, the battle of the dog of good breeding has been won, but the result will have to be consolidated—victory has to be won in every generation, there is no finality about it. The main danger of popularity is mass production, a method quite unsuited to dog breeding. Recent media publicity focussed on puppy farms has at last made the public aware of the appalling conditions under which some of our pedigree puppies are born and reared before being offered for sale. Not before time! The popularity of the pedigree dog as a pet will only continue if the dogs themselves give satisfaction to their owners as house dogs and companions.

The problems of rearing and managing show stock and pets are substantially the same, though the requirements of the pet owner may differ slightly from those of the breeder and exhibitor. Both, however, will demand a puppy which is healthy, well reared and which has a normally satisfactory temperament.

Fortunately, both for dog and owner, many of our best dogs do live as members of a household and develop a degree of intelligence and understanding, of loyalty and affection, impossible to dogs which lead a purely kennel life, almost cut off from human companionship and the pleasure and duties of a family.

The requirements of the pet owner are comparatively simple. He is not unduly concerned about technical show points, though he wants a dog he can be proud of as a definite specimen of its breed. He wants to be able to show its pedigree to his friends; he wants a dog which is healthy, good-tempered and reliable; he wants to be able to take his dog about with him happily, proudly and without anxiety. He does not want a weakling; he does not want a nervous dog, or a savage or even bad-tempered dog; he does not want to have to pay for postmen's trousers, or, worse still, legal costs against him for his dog's crimes. And the nicer he is, and the more of a dog lover he is, the greater the tragedy when the dog he has already grown to love goes wrong.

It must be said that much trouble is the fault of the owner, who often has no idea of how to look after or train a puppy, or even perhaps that a puppy needs training, just as a child does, and that the same methods of patience and affection produce the best results. Unfortunately, puppies are not all well reared, nor are they all bred from temperamentally sound stock, and they start life with a handicap. Breeders who sell puppies with these handicaps are not only wrong and cruel, they are stupid. Nothing is so easy to lose as a reputation, and nothing is so valuable to any breeder of livestock as a name for straight dealing.

The choice of breeding stock is considered at some length in Chapter Twelve.

Many breeders become breeders by accident as it were. They buy a pet and it turns out well, it is shown, does some winning and the enthusiast is born, or, as some people say, an incurable disease has been contracted!

The dog lover who buys a pet should always bear this possibility in mind, and should choose, or have chosen for him, a puppy, preferably a bitch, which will fulfil the basic requirements of all breeding stock, namely: to be a typical healthy and sound specimen of its breed, with a normal temperament, neither nervous nor aggressive, coming from good stock on both sides of the pedigree and, finally, bred by an experienced and reliable breeder.

The novice owner will learn much from buying a puppy rather than an older dog. He will form its habits and teach it all it must know as a member of the family, and as a show dog if this is to be its future. The writer's years of experience with dogs doubling the parts of companion and show dog have proved that there is no essential antagonism between the two roles; each complements the other. Confidence and affection between dog and owner are the essentials of success in both.

A bitch puppy, or puppies, is the wiser choice if there is any possibility of future breeding, or even if the puppy is to be a pet. The six-monthly heats are not difficult to manage, and bitches do not wander off as dogs do, for the latter are constantly attracted by the scent of the bitches in season which are often allowed loose at times when they should be kept at home.

The buyer who wishes to start breeding as soon as possible will probably buy older stock, bitches of perhaps ten months and upwards, but high prices are asked for good winning bitches of this age, and in many breeds they are very difficult to buy.

There is still another way of acquiring breeding stock, the method known as having a bitch 'on breeding terms'.

Breeding Terms

It is always wise to register this agreement with the Kennel Club.

The bitch is loaned from her owner to the second party in the transaction for any period of her lifetime, but not less than six months. The bitch must be registered by the Kennel Club, and no sale or transfer can take place during the continuance of the agreement. The two parties to the agreement must decide who is the owner in future of the bitch, which of the two parties to the loan is to be considered the breeder of any resultant puppies (in practice it is usually the owner who is loaning the bitch), and the duration of the arrangement. The selection of sire and payment of stud fee are matters of arrangement and should be stated in the agreement. The first party may stipulate for one or more puppies from the litter, and this must be stated, otherwise the Kennel Club will hold that all puppies belong to the breeder. It should also be stated which choices the first party should have, at what age, and by whom the choice is to be made and what action is to be taken in the event of only one puppy being born— as well as the responsibility for possible veterinary charges.

If this arrangement is registered with the Kennel Club and signed by both parties, any dispute arising out of this agreement will be considered by the Kennel Club and their decision will be final and binding on both parties to the loan.

Disagreement over breeding terms is one of the most usual sources of friction between breeders, who are given to making vague and verbal arrangements, of which there is no satisfactory proof and no means of enforcing.

It should be noted that the original owner of the bitch loaned on breeding terms is entitled to register any puppy or puppies due to him under the agreement, they are, in fact, his property from the moment of birth, and it follows that until the choice has been made, the rest of the litter cannot properly be registered.

To sum up:

1. Buy breeding stock from a reliable breeder and a carefully bred strain if possible.
2. Rear puppies carefully and see that they are both happy and healthy, the two are often interdependent.
3. Choose mates from the same strain, or from other strains as carefully bred, and consult the breeder on this point.
4. Choose a stud dog with a view to correcting the bitch's faults, by selecting one as nearly perfect as possible in the point in question.
5. Reinforce the bitch's good points by using a sire with the same.
6. See as many of the prospective sire's offspring as possible, and as many also of his ancestors, to gain an idea of what he may be expected to hand on to his progeny.

Heat, Mating and Pregnancy

The Stud Dog and Brood Bitch

In both sexes correct feeding, with a high protein diet, general good management and plenty of exercise, should be the rule, and a plea is made here for as natural a life as possible. A life, that is to say, not cut off from human companionship and all the doggy pleasures. A natural happy life will make a healthy and happy dog and will, undoubtedly, contribute to successful breeding.

A suitable environment and mode of life are important. This last is often neglected by small breeders, the numbers of whom have greatly increased since the war, and who keep both dogs and bitches as members of the family. Nothing could be more generally desirable, but the natural instinct for mating must be taken into account. This is among the entirely primitive and fundamental instincts and cannot be suppressed by any training. Much suffering may be caused to stud dogs if bitches in season are not kept strictly isolated from them. The instinct to mate is excited primarily by scent, not only by the vaginal discharge of the bitch, but also from her urine, and a dog who is constantly exposed to this stimulus may live in a state of real misery. Apart from the nuisance of constant fretting, howling and whining, the dog will usually lose his appetite entirely, and may lose flesh and condition in a very short time.

It is not advisable to keep dogs and bitches unless facilities are available for complete isolation of bitches in season. They should be kept in a kennel to which the dogs have no access at all; it is not enough to keep them separated by a fence, however safe this may be in preventing real contact. Dogs should not be allowed on ground used by bitches on heat, and with a keen stud dog an overall and rubber boots should be

15

used when the owner is attending to the bitches, and removed after use.

If a dog has been mated to one of his kennel mates, precautions should be doubled, as he will be constantly on the alert for sight and scent of her.

It is wise to separate dogs and bitches immediately the latter come in reason, even though during the first few days the dog may not be interested. One cannot be sure at which moment the bitch will become attractive to the dog, and once this has happened he will not easily settle down again. As is pointed out elsewhere in this book there is another drawback when dogs are left with bitches in the early stages of their heat; constant reproof may be needed to prevent the undue interest of the dog, even though mating is not yet possible, and this is very likely to affect his use at stud. Dogs are creatures of habit, and when a dog has been frequently scolded for his interest in a bitch it is more than likely to affect his reactions to the bitches brought to him for mating.

It is true, of course, that dogs vary greatly in temperament. Some are not stimulated at all except during the few days of the heat when mating could normally take place, but these are probably few in number and the scent of a bitch in season is likely to excite the average stud dog.

Like the stud dog, the brood bitch should be as good an example of her breed as possible. The healthier and more normal the life she leads the better, especially in the matter of exercise, for lack of this retards all the functions; moreover, strong and vigorous muscles make whelping easier. Like the stud dog, the brood bitch should never be allowed to become soft and fat.

It is important that before she is mated a bitch should be free from worms. Routine treatment for worms should be carried out two or three times a year but an extra dose when she is first coming into season prior to mating is sound management.

Heat

The bitch comes in season at fairly regular intervals of approximately six months, though a longer interval is by no means uncommon. In some breeds, such as the Basenji, which have a shorter history of domestication, the interval is usually twelve months, as in the primitive dog.

Even though normally regular, an individual bitch may have her heat delayed. Very cold weather is often responsible for this. It is an interesting fact that the well-known American authority, Whitney, believes the influence of light to be more important than that of temperature in stimulating the onset of oestrum.

Nature has ordained that animals in the wild state should have their litters in the spring, when weather conditions are favourable and the young stock can have the advantage of sun and warmth to facilitate growth. Domestication has altered this rhythm; two heats a year are now normal. With modern feeding and husbandry most bitches could adequately cope with two litters in one year provided the process did not continue. At least a year's rest would then be advisable. Toy breeds and those with large heads are frequently mated on their first heat, the theory being that the bones are more pliable and whelping difficulties are less likely to occur. This is acceptable providing the bitch is not turned into a breeding machine and is given adequate rest after her second litter, if this follows at the next heat. It is also extremely important to ensure that she is sufficiently mature at the time of her first season to be able to cope with pregnancy and motherhood. The age of the first heat and the time between heats can be very variable. Toys and small breeds mature earlier and can come into season before they are six months old. Giant breeds, Danes and Wolfhounds, will frequently go to 15 or even 18 months without showing signs of a season.

Abnormalities of oestrum are not at all uncommon. The outward sign of this function, namely discharge of mucus and blood from the uterus, may be totally absent, or scanty, denoting some abnormality of the reproductive cycle. On the other hand, the periods may be excessive, prolonged or liable to occur at too-frequent intervals, which equally indicates some disorder, either of the generative organs themselves or of the system in general.

A decline in the reproductive function may be due to hormone defects, involving diminution or absence of the glandular secretions initiating and regulating the sexual function. Conversely, overactive glands will result in prolonged or too-frequent heats.

Local inflammatory conditions of the genital organs are likely to interfere with the normal heat, including such conditions as ovarian diseases or the chronically inflamed condition of the uterus known as chronic metritis caused by both bacteria (E. coli) and BHS infections and also viruses.

Other diseases of the genital organs may give rise to bleeding of an irregular character, not to be confused with physiological oestrum. Such diseases are growths of various kinds, especially malignant growths, of which irregular bleeding may be the first sign.

It is only during the period of heat that the normal bitch will allow herself to be mated, or that the normal dog evinces any sexual interest in her. Moreover, only during a few days of this period, usually four or five, does mating take place.

The Normal Heat

Heat is heralded by an enlargement of the vaginal orifice, with some swelling, which may be very noticeable or hardly obvious, accompanied by mucous discharge. This stage usually lasts for some days, even a week or more, though it must be stressed that in some bitches these preliminaries are so slight as to be hardly noticeable. They are followed by marked swelling and hardening of the region with a bloodstained discharge which finally has the appearance of pure blood. This may be very copious, but varies greatly in amount with different individuals. By about the end of the first week after the red colour has been noticed the discharge is usually at its height, and the swelling and hardening of the vagina at their maximum. As the heat progresses, the discharge becomes less copious, and the vulva begins to soften. This softening is a sign that the time for mating is approaching. In the third week of the heat all the signs begin to diminish, and by the end of this period the organs will have returned to normal.

In most bitches the duration of the heat is about three weeks, though in some it may last longer. The first week is

occupied by the waxing stage; during the second week the heat
is at its height, and mating usually takes place towards the end
of the second week, or early in the third, which is then devoted
to the stage of waning.

The actual time of acceptance, during which the bitch can
be mated, depends on the breed and the individual; it may be
early or late. Bitches have been mated as early as the fourth
day of the season, and as late as the nineteenth or twentieth, in
both cases successfully. Also, the time may vary with the same
bitch on different occasions. I have myself owned a bitch who
was mated twice, each time on the thirteenth day. On the third
occasion she would have nothing to do with the dog until the
nineteenth day, when she made it clear that she was ready to
be mated, and in due course produced a litter of eleven.

It is often stated that the proper time for mating is when the
red discharge has practically ceased; this is by no means an
infallible rule, for in many bitches the red discharge will persist for the entire period of the heat, and if the owner waits
until it has stopped the possible time will have passed.

There is only one rule for fruitful mating: it must take place
when the bitch indicates by her behaviour that she is ready.
Rule-of-thumb methods are useless. There is no doubt that
many bitches fail because breeders have fixed ideas about correct dates. The indications mentioned are valuable signs,
perhaps the most useful being the softening of the vagina.

From the onset of her heat, and especially after the first
week, the bitch is attractive to dogs. This attraction is a matter
of scent; any bitch who is taken out on the roads leaves a trail of
scent, which will attract any males who come across it. It is a
safe rule, therefore, to keep a bitch at home on her own
ground during this time, for it is the only way of avoiding
unwanted suitors. If she has a safely enclosed paddock to run
in, so much the better, but even then she should never be left
alone as only an exceptional fence can keep out a determined
dog. It has been known for a dog separated by a linked-mesh
fencing from a bitch in season to mate her through the obstacle. Exercise is bound to be restricted during these few
weeks, since running at large is out of the question; a healthy,
well-exercised bitch will suffer no harm from the enforced
confinement. It is hardly necessary to say that if she must be

taken out on the roads it should be on a strong collar and lead or chain, for not only is the dog attracted to her but she herself has the urge to be mated, and if she escapes during the crucial days a misalliance is certain. The writer is constantly surprised by the haphazard, careless methods so often used to safeguard even valuable bitches from unwanted suitors; it is small wonder that many mis-matings occur.

It must be stressed that during her season, and especially during the few days of maximum intensity, the bitch must be kept in such security that neither she herself can break out nor any dog get in. Dogs will readily dig under wire, or get in through open windows, and bitches are liable to get out, though if the bitch has not been allowed out to leave her scent, dangers from the dog are greatly reduced.

The use of pungently scented preparations applied to the hindquarters of the bitch is very common, especially among owners of pets. The writer has no personal experience of this practice, as her bitches are always isolated during heat, but several owners of stud dogs have remarked that their dogs become accustomed to these scents, and in fact soon associate them with a bitch on heat, reacting accordingly.

During her heat the bitch is usually rather more affectionate than usual. She may at the same time be inclined to irritability with other bitches, especially in the early days, when they find her scent attractive, but when she herself has not fully developed the sexual urge. There is no reason why a healthy bitch should be at all indisposed during this time; she suffers no ill effects from this entirely natural process, but it is wise to see that she does not get a chill as this might interfere with the normal course of the season.

False Pregnancy

This condition is quite common in bitches. It is known by a variety of names, phantom pregnancy, pseudo pregnancy, pseudocyesis. After a bitch has been in heat the hormonal changes that occur are similar, irrespective of whether she is pregnant or not. During pregnancy certain hormones, particularly progesterone are secreted in greater quantity. If this occurs in a bitch that is unmated or has been mated and failed to conceive, false pregnancy can result and the signs can vary from a mild broodiness to a full blown state of false pregnancy when the bitch develops copious milk supplies, makes a nest and sometimes experiences bouts of nervousness or even aggression. Thus a phantom pregnancy is really an exaggeration of the normal hormonal changes occuring after a heat. The signs occur about two months after the heat, which is approximately when the bitch would be having puppies. Milk will often increase in quantity for a further three or four weeks and then the signs gradually subside. In the wild state and also in kennels bitches in a phantom pregnancy serve a useful purpose since they will happily rear and feed orphan puppies. Bitches prone to phantom pregnancies will tend to have them following each heat and they often increase in severity to the stage where sterilisation is the only answer. If the bitch does not come into season she will not develop a false pregnancy.

The best treatment initially is to ignore the condition but ensure that surrogate puppies in the form of slippers, toys etc, are removed from the nest. In this way the signs will disappear that much sooner. The bitch should be encouraged to exercise but if she becomes aggressive, hormone treatment and sometimes sedation has to be prescribed by the veterinary surgeon.

Signs of Readiness for Mating

When the bitch is ready for mating she usually shows this very plainly, especially in the company of another bitch. These signs have already been described but may be mentioned again as they are important. The bitch will stand rigidly, with hindquarters outstretched and tail held aside when sniffed at by her companions. She will often play the part of the dog and mount another bitch, and she will make it thoroughly obvious that her sexual instincts are aroused. With most bitches this stage lasts for at least three or four days, or even longer, though there are exceptional bitches with whom it lasts only a few hours. The maximum intensity is usually about thirty-six to forty-eight hours from the time when she will first stand, and this is the most favourable time for mating her.

The usual practice is to take or send the bitch to the dog.

Owners of bitches are advised to accompany them on these occasions, or to send them with a reliable person. In the first place the bitch will be more at her ease with someone she knows, especially if she is a maiden, and therefore the mating will be less of an ordeal for her. In addition to this aspect, unless the owner of the sire is known, it is as well in these days of commercial breeding to be certain that the sire selected is actually the one used. It is not unknown for another dog to deputize for a popular sire—without the knowledge of the owner of the bitch, needless to say. For the same reason, in dealing with strangers the owner should be present at the mating. Sometimes owners of stud dogs refuse to agree to this, possibly on the grounds that bitches may be more amenable without their owners, especially in the case of spoilt pets, but the owner certainly has the right to be present, if he wishes, at any rate until it has been proved that his presence is hindering rather than helping. He can then be sure that his bitch is not roughly handled.

It does occasionally happen that a dog and bitch refuse to mate unless they are alone, and are allowed to manage for themselves. If they are friendly with each other there is no reason against this; a quiet watch can be kept through a convenient window.

Excessive busy-ness and over-handling on the part of the owners during mating is as much to be deprecated as over-handling in the show ring; some people forget that the pair have any ideas of their own in the matter, and undue interference may easily deter what would otherwise be a normal natural proceeding. A young stud dog, however, should be taught at his first few matings not to resent a minimum amount of handling, at times necessary with difficult bitches. If not taught this early, he may refuse assistance even when it is necessary.

The bitch should always have some hours' rest after mating; it is unwise to take her off at once, either on foot or by car.

It is sometimes possible for the dog to visit the bitch, the ideal arrangement. The bitch, especially if she is a maiden, will be happier and more at ease in her own home, and will be able to rest quietly afterwards in her own bed. The obvious drawback to this course is the possible uncertainty of the correct day for the mating. If the owner of the bitch can arrange a visit from the dog on the correct day there is everything in favour of this proceeding. Unfortunately many owners of bitches have only the vaguest ideas on this subject, often being unable to say on exactly which day the bitch came in season. Such owners are inclined to send the bitch off early in her heat, leaving everything else to the owner of the sire. If the bitch be sent away for mating, this should be done a day or two before the day on which mating is likely, and not at the onset of her heat. Owners of stud dogs do not charge for the keep of a bitch for a few days but if she has to be kept for a week or longer it would be quite in order to charge a boarding fee.

Whatever arrangements are made should be in good time and the owner of the sire notified as soon as the bitch comes on heat.

Should an unaccompanied bitch be sent by train it is essential to send her in a strong and roomy travelling box, securely locked, and never in a basket or hamper, out of which she could chew her way. Nor, needless to say, should she ever be sent loose on a collar and lead. The box should be well ventilated, and be large enough for her to be able to stand upright and lie down comfortably. There should be a good thick bed of straw. No bitch should be sent on a journey so long as to cause her any suffering, whether from hunger, thirst or confinement. In these days of delayed travelling any really long journey, and especially one involving change of trains, may result in lengthy delay, and should be avoided.

There should be duplicate keys to the box, one being sent well in advance to the owner of the sire. Telephone the stud owner at the time of despatch, stating time of arrival. The stud fee does not cover the return carriage of the bitch; her owner should make arrangements to pay this.

Stud fees should be paid at the time of mating. The stud fee is paid for the service of the dog, irrespective of whether it results in a litter. It is the common practice to allow a second service without further fee, should the first prove unfruitful. In dealing with strangers it is wise to have any such understanding clearly stated in writing. Stud fees vary largely. They range from £20–30 up to several hundred pounds, according to the show success and popularity of the sire. It should be stressed that since the stud fee is a small item in the cost of rearing a litter, economy in this direction is misguided. It does not follow, of course, that the dog standing at the highest fee is necessarily the best mate for any particular bitch, but no question of fee should deter the serious breeder from using the dog which is most suitable.

Arrangements in Lieu of Stud Fees

The most satisfactory plan is undoubtedly to pay the fee and to assume no further commitments to the owner of the sire. It is not uncommon, however, for other arrangements to be made. The owner of the sire may take a puppy in lieu of the stud fee, or make any other plan mutually agreeable. In former days a puppy was considered to be the equivalent of a stud fee, but this is not always now the case. It may happen that the services of a particular dog are in such request that the owner of the bitch is prepared to agree to any terms in order to use him. New breeders, on the other hand, whose puppies are not in such demand may be glad to have a puppy already disposed of in this way. Whatever arrangements of this kind are made should be stated in writing, and if one or more puppies are to be taken in lieu of the fee it should be definitely stated which choice, if any, the owner of the sire is to have. The arrangements should be drawn up to cover such possibilities as there being only one puppy, and all other contingencies.

The owner of the stud dog has certain responsibilities, both moral and legal. It is a moral responsibility that the dog shall be fertile, and a proved sire, unless it is clearly understood that the mating is an experimental one, and it is incumbent on the owner not to allow the dog to be so over-used that his sexual power is diminished. He assumes legal responsibility for the safe keeping of the bitch while in his charge, and is expected to take all precautions for her safety, and the additional ones necessary at this time to ensure that no other dog has access to her.

Normal Mating

Mating is a natural process; it should present no difficulties with a normal dog and bitch ready for service. It is better not to

feed either within a short time of service, and both should have
a good opportunity for relieving themselves before mating. It
is especially important that the bitch should have had her
bowels opened; a loaded rectum may render the act of
mating uncomfortable.

It is usually more convenient to mate the dogs in some
room or building in which there is plenty of space for the preliminary play and courtship, but in which the dogs can be controlled if necessary, and from which they cannot escape. The
room should contain nothing which might injure the animals
in their play. When they are known to be friendly, a preliminary run together outside may often be an advantage in
accustoming the pair to each other.

The dogs should be introduced on leads, and it is advisable
for both to wear collars. Before releasing them it is wise to
make sure that the bitch will not be unfriendly, or snap at the
dog. Some dogs are so deterred by a display of bad temper on
the part of the bitch that they will refuse to have anything more
to do with her. Real bad temper or even savagery must be dis-
tinguished from the playful semi-snapping which often
occurs, which is in effect a sort of token resistance and is well
understood by both animals to be no more than this.

Once it is clear that there is to be no bad temper, the pair
should be released and allowed to play together. This preliminary play is part of the process of mating, the bitch displaying coyness, the dog making advances. When her
reactions show that she is ready—that is, standing with hindquarters braced and tail held aside—the dog may be allowed
to mount her, but until this stage is reached he should not be
allowed to do so. It may take a little time for the bitch to reach
this point, and the dog should not be allowed to worry her
unduly until she is obviously ready.

Stud dogs vary very much in their behaviour. The ideal dog
is keen, but not so keen that he omits the preliminary state of
courtship. One sometimes meets a dog so keen that he allows
the bitch no time to get used to him, and goes straight ahead
with the actual mating. Such a dog may be very difficult with
an inexperienced bitch, who is likely to be more coy than
a matron. She may be frightened by the dog's rough
advances.

It should be emphasized that the stage of courtship should

not be hurried by the attendants; it is actually part of the physiological process of mating. One has seen bitches, even maidens, seized and held immovable from the start, without any chance to accustom themselves to the dog. They are bewildered and panic-stricken, poor things, and do their best to resist, and it is hardly surprising that many of them fail to conceive.

It is often advised that a bitch should be muzzled for mating. There is no need for this as a routine. To a bitch unaccustomed to a muzzle it is frightening and distracting; she is likely to concentrate far more on getting rid of the detested thing than on the business in hand. It is useful, however, to have a muzzle or a piece of broad tape handy in case of need.

Once the bitch is standing firmly, the owner should steady her by the collar, and if, when the dog mounts her, she tends to let the hindquarters sag they should be supported by a hand (or a knee in case of large breeds), keeping the stifle joint extended. The moment of penetration may be painful to a maiden bitch; she will often give a sharp cry and instinctively attempt to move forward away from the dog. This can be stopped by a firm hold on the collar. The dog will clasp her round the abdomen with his forelegs and will remain thus for a short time. He will then be ready to turn himself; if necessary, he may be helped to do this by lifting one foreleg over the bitch's back, so that both are on the same side. The corresponding hind leg may then be lifted gently over the hindquarters of the bitch. During the tie the erectile tissue forming the bulb of the penis is locked within the female passage by the strong muscles of the vulva thus preventing withdrawal of the penis. Since this can last up to an hour in extreme cases, obviously in the wild state the two animals were very vulnerable to attack. In consequence the dog turns so that it is standing bottom to bottom with the bitch and thus both can defend themselves more easily. A full description of the tie appears in Captain Portman-Graham's book, *The Mating and Whelping of Dogs*, published in the Popular Dogs series. If the bitch is big in relation to the dog, it may be necessary to straddle her hind legs out slightly. All actions should be gentle and unhurried, and the pair should then be standing back to back, comfortably on all four feet.

With the tie established, it is wise to steady both dog and bitch by the collar, otherwise they will wander about, the one dragging the other. Camp-stools can be a great comfort to attendants at this stage, which may last for well over half an hour. Small dogs are often mated on a table, which is more comfortable for the assistants though perhaps not as satisfactory for the dogs, whose preliminary freedom of movement is restricted.

When the dog withdraws, the bitch should be taken away first and left quietly in her bed to rest. Both dog and bitch may be given a meal and a drink after mating.

To return to the dog; if his efforts at mating meet with no initial success he should be restrained from further attempts until the engorged tissues subside. As long as the bulb of erectile tissue is still swollen he is unable to penetrate, and further attempts should be stopped until the swelling has subsided.

Difficult and Abnormal Mating

Many difficult matings are the result of the unreadiness of the bitch. The reason for this is the physiological one that the generative organs are not in a state to render conception likely, or even possible, for reasons already considered. Similarly, obstructions of varying kinds in the vagina of the bitch may render mating impossible. In cases where anything of the sort is suspected, attempts at mating will only cause suffering and injury to the bitch, and veterinary advice should be sought at once.

Disparity of Size

This is a not uncommon factor in preventing easy mating. If the dog is either much bigger or much smaller than the bitch the act of mating may be impossible unless one partner can be raised to the level of the other. This is easier when the bitch is the smaller, as she is the more passive partner and can be induced to stand on a board raised some inches from the ground. If the dog must be raised, a board is not satisfactory as it tends to be slippery, and he will find it difficult to get a foothold. It is never easy to get a dog to stand on the raised surface because, as the active partner, he is on the move. Perhaps the best form of platform is one or two thick coconut mats, for the rough surface enables him to get a perfect footing. Many dogs are, however, most reluctant to be placed in this way.

Generally speaking, it is not advisable to mate animals of great difference in size. Should the bitch be much the smaller, relatively large puppies may result, which is likely to give rise to difficulties in whelping. Ideally, the dog should be a couple of inches taller than the bitch, and as this often is the case mating usually occurs without any trouble on this score. In the establishment of miniature and toy breeds from larger varieties, the usual practice is to mate a dog of small stock, and himself of the smallest size, to a bitch big enough to be safe in whelping, and also from small-bred stock.

The unwillingness of the bitch has already been considered. It need only be said that the large majority of bitches in most breeds are willing provided that they are mated at the right time.

Frigidity

This condition will be dealt with more fully in the following chapter. There are a certain number of bitches who are never willing to be mated, whether from constitutional frigidity or other reasons. A bitch who, for instance, has been badly frightened, roughly handled, or hurt at her first attempt at mating may never forget it, and thereafter refuse the dog. These bitches of all classes present a problem— the owner has to decide whether to allow them to follow their natural inclinations or to mate them by force. The method of enforced mating will be described in the next chapter. It can be justified only after the most utmost patience has been used to bring about a natural mating at a time when the bitch is known to be ready, and for special reasons, such as the fact that the progeny of the bitch is essential to a breeding plan, but it should be borne in mind that the condition of fridigity is more than likely to be inherited by the progeny.

The Indifferent Dog

It has been said that dogs vary in their reaction to the bitch. Some may be diffident owing to bad management, to the practice of allowing bitches in the early part of their heat to be with dogs, and to the constant reprimands the dog receives for his entirely natural interest.

Some dogs, although attracted by the bitch and ready to indulge in courtship, will refuse to mate, a state of affairs doubtless due to a lack of balance in the internal secretions governing sexual behaviour and capacity.

A sickly dog, or one excessively fat, is also likely to be lethargic, but restoration to health should remedy the first, and in the second dieting and exercise to reduce weight will usually be successful, always provided that the excessive fat is not a symptom of glandular deficiency, and in particular thyroid deficiency, in which case steps must be taken to deal with this.

Dual Conceptions

The possibility of a bitch conceiving to two different dogs in the same heat has been much discussed. There is no reason why this should not occur in a species which produces multiple offspring at one birth. Much evidence exists to suggest that it does in fact take place.

The usual sequence of events is for a planned mating to occur, and for the bitch to escape a day or two later to be again mated by another dog, either a mongrel or one of her own kennel-mates of the same breed, or, of course, a pure-bred dog of a different breed.

If she has been mated by two dogs of her own breed it may be impossible to say which of the two is the sire of any individual puppy, unless the interval has been so long that the progeny of the second mating are obviously immature at birth. If, as the puppies grow, some marked feature of appearance or some trick of behaviour peculiar to one of the dogs is noticed, this may identify the sire. The progeny of a misalliance will be dealt with in a succeeding paragraph.

Kennel Club regulations for the registration of dogs lay

down that if a bitch has been served by two dogs in the same heat, the names of both dogs must be given when the puppies are registered.

Second Services

Differences of opinion exist as to the advisability of a second service. It is the practice in some kennels to mate twice as a routine, with an interval of from twenty-four to forty-eight hours between services. Should the first mating have been entirely satisfactory, the bitch ready and eager, the dog keen, the tie of normal length, there seems to be no advantage in this proceeding. Should any doubt exist about the bitch's readiness or should the tie have failed or been unduly short, a second mating on the following day may ensure a litter. The interval between services should never be a long one; twenty-four hours is the ideal and forty-eight the limit. Conception may result from both matings, and should the interval between them be long the puppies from the second mating, born as they almost certainly will be with those resulting from the first mating, may be prejudiced by their prematurity. My own practice is to mate the animals once only, providing the first service is natural and easy. It has proved successful alike with experienced stud dogs, with youngsters mated for the first time and with dogs after a prolonged interval since the last occasion.

Litters Arising from a Misalliance

The physical appearance of puppies born as the result of a mating between two pure-bred dogs of different varieties does not necessarily give any hint of mixed parentage in the individual puppy. The puppies of such a mating may be of two kinds:

1. They may show evidence of crossing at birth, or after an interval.
2. They may at birth appear to be pure-bred specimens of either or both breeds, and may retain the appearance of pure breeding throughout life. If they are bred from,

evidence of their mixed ancestry will occur in the next generation when segregation takes place according to Mendel's Law.

Such puppies may be, and often are, sold as pure-bred specimens by ignorant or unscrupulous people.

Discredited Opinions

Many views on breeding subjects have had to be abandoned with increasing knowledge, among them are:

Telegony. By this term we understand the supposed influence of a previous sire, exercised on the offspring of a bitch by a subsequent and different sire. This view was widely held during the nineteenth century, and was supported by various happenings which appeared to lend colour to it, but which have no validity in the light of more accurate observation and more knowledge of heredity. But even nowadays it is not unknown for dog breeders to believe that a bitch which has contracted a misalliance will never be able to have pure-bred puppies by a dog of her own breed. By what means the persistent influence of the first mate is maintained is not explained. It would be just as reasonable to suggest that the first pure-bred dog to which any bitch is mated exerts a permanent influence on all her later litters. If this were indeed the case, a single mating to an outstanding dog would solve the breeder's problems for the entire breeding life of the bitch. It is hardly necessary to say that there is no foundation for belief in telegony.

Pre-Natal Influence. This is another of the hoary beliefs which have no foundation in fact. It has been a very popular myth, in human as well as in animal breeding. A birth-mark, for instance, in a child is still often held to be due to some event occurring during pre-natal life, often a frightening experience of the mother.

When animals of a certain colour have been wished for it has been the practice to put the pregnant dam among those of the desired colour, in the expectation of influencing the colour of the unborn progeny.

The increase in knowledge which the science of heredity has brought about shows that there is no foundation for this view. In fact, colour and all attributes are determined by heredity factors from parents and forbears, acting in accordance with the laws of genetics. The mechanism of transmission is understood. In many cases, notably those of colour transmission in cattle and some breeds of dogs, it has been investigated and has been proved to take place in exact accordance with the known theories of heredity. Much work remains to be done on these lines.

Predetermination of Sex.　　Many theories have been advanced, and are still widely held, concerning procedures by which the sex of puppies can be influenced. One of the most favoured is the view that by mating a bitch early in her heat a preponderance of bitch puppies will result, on the grounds that if a bitch be mated early it argues a large number of dogs are about, and that Nature will therefore redress the balance in favour of bitches. And the reverse is presumed to hold, namely that if a bitch be mated late in her heat it supposes few dogs are about, and that again the balance will be altered in favour of dogs.

The section on genetics in this book will quickly convince you that there is no foundation for this or any similar theory and no way is yet known by which either sex can be produced at will although the advances made in molecular biology and genetic typing may radically alter this in the not too distant future.

Pregnancy

The period between service and whelping is on the average sixty-two to sixty-three days. It may be several days less in small breeds or large litters, but it is unlikely that puppies premature by more than a week will survive.

Gestation may be prolonged by several days; cases have been recorded in which whelping has not occurred until after ten weeks from mating. These must be considered as most unusual.

The delay of a day or two may be explained by supposing

that conception did not take place on the actual date of mating. This is quite possible, for active sperms have been recovered from the vagina of a bitch several days after service. Most cases of delay of more than a few days, and all those within my own experience, indicate some abnormal condition which requires investigation. This point will be further considered 'in the chapter on whelping.

Signs of Pregnancy

Definite signs will not as a rule be present for some weeks after mating, though this will vary with the individual. It may be as long as six or seven weeks before a certain diagnosis can be made, and cases have been recorded where doubt has existed until the birth of the puppies has settled it. On the other hand there may be reasonable certainty as early as the third week.

Progressive Abdominal Enlargement. This is the most noticeable sign; it begins with a slight filling out in the flanks. Should the litter be small, this sign may not be evident until about the fifth or sixth week, but in cases of really big litters it is usually seen by about the fourth week or even earlier. The enlargement, which should progress steadily, is naturally noticed sooner in matrons who have had several litters, owing to the greater slackness of the abdominal wall.

During the last weeks of pregnancy the uterus, which previously lay along the spinal column, drops into the abdominal cavity, and is much more obvious. The enlargement of the abdomen in a bitch which has been mated may be due to other unrelated causes, and cannot therefore in itself be taken as an unmistakable sign of pregnancy.

Alterations of Behaviour. Slight or marked changes in the normal behaviour of a bitch are quite usual in pregnancy. The lively, boisterous manner often becomes quieter. Appetite, too, is often increased and in the later stages will sometimes be ravenous, though it may happen that in the early stages the bitch is inclined to be finicky over food.

Cessation of the Discharge after Mating.   It is sometimes believed that in the case of successful mating the uterine discharge ceases abruptly after union, and that this cessation can be taken as a sign that conception has occurred. In my own experience this sign is not reliable. Bitches have continued to bleed after mating for the duration of the heat, subsequently giving birth to large and normal litters. In other cases the discharge has ceased immediately after mating. No reliance can therefore be placed on the duration of bleeding as a sign of pregnancy. A point I have noticed, however, in many bitches is that, whereas in unmated bitches the vulva returns to normal when the heat is over, in the pregnant bitch it never quite returns to the quiescent state but remains slightly enlarged.

Examination of the Abdomen.   Some experienced veterinary surgeons are satisfied that they can feel the developing foetuses very early in pregnancy. This will depend on the tactile skill of the observer, and also on the degree of muscular relaxation of the abdominal wall. Such a degree is not likely to be achieved without the help of a general anaesthetic, and breeders will be well advised not to attempt to determine the number of puppies by trying to count them in the abdomen.

X-Ray Examination.   In the later stages of pregnancy it is possible to establish the number of whelps by radiography. Due to the hazards of radiation this should only be carried out on the possibly pregnant bitch as a last resort and all other methods of pregnancy detection have failed. In other species today, particularly sheep, ultrasound appears to offer a safer alternative to positive pregnancy diagnosis. In the years to come we may well see the increased use of this technique in bitches once it has been proven to be totally safe for both mother and foetus.

Enlargement of the Teats.   This sign is usually noticed at about the sixth week. In the case of bitches who have had a previous litter such an enlargement usually takes place during the last two weeks of the gestation period, whether the bitch has been mated or not, so that although in maidens it is a fairly reliable sign it is by no means so in matrons.

Movement of the Unborn Puppies. This is the one unmistakable sign of pregnancy. It is usually seen during the last week of gestation, especially when the bitch is relaxed and lying on her side. It may happen that in very large litters the puppies are so closely packed together that little movement is seen, but in litters of normal size it is usually very obvious and is sometimes very vigorous.

Abortion. Natural abortion in the bitch is rare; the cause is usually severe illness, violence of some kind, endocrine abnormality in which one of the internal secretions governing pregnancy fails to function, or another is over-active, or a hereditary tendency to abortion, probably brought about by the same cause. Exhausting exercise, violent jumping, and other unaccustomed and strenuous exertions should be avoided. The bitch should not be allowed to play with rough companions, and accidental blows or knocks should be carefully guarded against. I do not believe that any ordinary activity, such as going up and down stairs in a house-trained bitch, is in the least likely to cause abortion, unless some other cause for it is already present.

Unwanted pregnancies can be aborted by a veterinary surgeon, with the use of synthetic hormonal products, provided these are administered within approximately 48 hours of mating. They should not be relied upon however as an antidote for carelessness since they do carry side effects.

To return to the management of the pregnant bitch. Following service it will be necessary to prevent any other dog having access to her for the remainder of her heat. After being mated most bitches evince the strongest desire for a repetition of the experience, and it is, if possible, even more necessary to guard her carefully at this stage than before mating has taken place. Once her heat is over, the bitch should resume normal life and should not be treated in any way as an invalid.

Feeding of the Bitch in Whelp

It cannot be too often repeated that puppy rearing begins not with the birth of the litter, but at the time of mating the bitch, and even before, for conception will depend to some extent on the state of the bitch's nutrition, and on the presence of the essential elements of diet.

To put the matter at its simplest: during the entire nine weeks which elapse between conception and whelping the bitch has to supply from her own bloodstream all the constituents needed to form the bones, muscles, nerves and entire bodies of a number of puppies, varying from three or four to ten or twelve. The actual total weight of a large litter at birth may be seven or eight pounds. The developing whelps can grow satisfactorily only if the bitch is able to supply them with adequate amounts of all necessary substances, and this she does from her own diet by means of the circulation. A bitch whose diet is deficient in protein, calcium or any other essential substance, will supply these as far as she is able from her own body substance, but in such a case her reserves, and her own essential requirements, will be gravely depleted and her constitution will deteriorate in a marked manner. When her reserves are exhausted the puppies will suffer a serious deficiency in nutrition. The developing puppies derive their nutriment through the placenta, or afterbirth, from the maternal blood. An interchange of foetal and maternal blood takes place in the placenta, the blood of the foetus absorbing the substances needed for growth and discarding into the maternal blood the waste products accumulated by the growing embryo. It will be clear, therefore, that in order to provide an adequate supply of food material the bitch herself must be fed amply and correctly, and that her diet must contain plentiful amounts of bone- and body-building food, together with the vitamins necessary to health, and the essential minerals. It is interesting that veterinary research has shown that calves born to cows which received large additional amounts of Vitamin A in the weeks preceding calving were found to have a considerably higher percentage of this vitamin stored in their livers than calves of cows not similarly treated, and this Vitamin A concentration undoubtedly has a great influence on the health and resistance to infection of the new-born animal during the critical first week or two of life.

Ample food does not mean that the bitch should be overfed, and especially it does not mean that she should be stuffed with food of high bulk but little nutritive value. The ideal diet for the pregnant bitch is a plentiful supply of meat, raw and fresh if possible, a good wholemeal cereal, and such additions as eggs, cod-liver or halibut-liver oil, and extra bone-forming material. The latter may well be given in the form of calcium, of which there are many excellent preparations on the market. Stress (Phillips Yeast Products Ltd) and Pet Cal (Beecham Animal Health) are widely available. With both of these supplementation with cod-liver oil or halibut-liver oil is unnecessary.

Quality rather than quantity should be the main concern and a concentrated food such as meat, with its high protein value, is much more useful than large amounts of carbohydrate food.

For the first few weeks of pregnancy the bitch's appetite will usually be normal; she may be finicky over her food, though this is unusual. For the first four weeks her normal diet should suffice, providing it contains plenty of meat and a daily supply of vitamins in the form of cod-liver oil and a yeast preparation. As pregnancy advances, and the unborn puppies grow, as they do very rapidly from the fifth week onward, the bitch's appetite will increase as will her abdominal pressure. Therefore nourishing food containing high levels of good quality protein and fat rather than bulky starchy foods should be offered. Feeding smaller meals more frequently is also advisable. Vitamin supplements should be included at this time but it is worthwhile seeking veterinary advice since overdosing with vitamin preparations can have a deleterious affect. Eggs on a two or three times weekly basis are also useful at this time.

As pregnancy advances and the bitch becomes heavier it may be wise to divide the food into three meals daily instead of two. Pressure within the abdomen is great; the stomach is likely to be compressed, and the distension caused by a large meal may be very uncomfortable or even painful. The appetite of a healthy bitch is extremely large at this time, and the more concentrated the food the better, for the bitch will obtain the maximum of nourishment with the minimum of bulk. This should be the aim of any system of feeding the pregnant bitch. She should never be allowed to become too fat. Excess fat predisposes to difficult whelping and to feeble puppies. A bitch who puts all her food 'on her own back' does not usually nurture her puppies as well as one who remains reasonably thin, and diet should be arranged to increase the protein in the form of lean meat and fish, which does not dispose to fatness.

During the last few hours of her pregnancy the bitch will probably refuse all food, and as by then whelping is imminent this will be considered in the following chapter.

Bowel Action in Pregnancy

It is particularly necessary during the in-whelp period that the bitch should have regular evacuations of the bowels. She has to cope not only with her own waste products but also with those thrown off by the litter, and any interference with elimination is likely to affect both dam and puppies.

No difficulty is experienced during the early weeks, but it may happen that constipation is troublesome during the last few weeks, especially if the bitch be very heavy.

If aperients should be necessary it is important to give mild ones; no drug should be used which is likely to irritate the intestine. Malt extract may be tried; it has a definite laxative value and is a useful addition to the diet. Liquid paraffin is useful as a laxative but it should not be overdone since it prevents absorption of oil-soluble vitamins A, D and E from the intestine. Devoid of taste and smell, it can usefully be added to the food with dogs that are difficult to dose. Doses range from a teaspoonful to a tablespoonful, (5–20 ml) according to the size of animal. In excess it leaks from the anus and can soil the coat. If it is ineffective Petrolagar or Agerol can be tried, but it is probably more prudent to consult your veterinary surgeon.

Plentiful supplies of clean drinking water are essential for health and also for helping bowel action, and should never be forgotten.

Exercise during Pregnancy

There is no doubt about the importance of exercise at all stages of a dog's life, but its importance during pregnancy is apt to be overlooked. There is no reason why any normal, healthy bitch should not take her usual exercise through the greater part of the period, and exercise of a more limited kind right up to the date of whelping. During the later weeks she should be allowed to go at her own pace, and should never be forced, and jumping and violent play should be prohibited. Walking on a lead is no real exercise while the bitch is still active, but as she becomes large and heavy it may be enough for her, provided the walks are far enough to stretch her limbs well and set her circulation going. Freedom to run at large should be provided during the early stages of gestation; this is essential for good muscular development. It must be remembered that the muscles clothing the skeleton are not the only muscles present in the body. The internal organs, such as the intestine, contain muscles, the uterus consists almost entirely of muscle, as does the heart itself. These internal muscles are not voluntary, such as those of the skeleton, in which movement is initiated by the will. They are termed involuntary muscles; their movement persists througout life, and is initiated and controlled by a complex nervous mechanism. Nevertheless their tone and efficiency depend on a proper supply of blood circulating through them, and this is influenced by exercise, so that regular activity will strengthen them just as it does the skeletal muscles. Therefore let the bitch have regular and adequate exercise throughout the whole of her pregnancy; it will help to keep her bowels regular, it will improve her circulation and it will strengthen her muscles for the task of giving birth to her young.

Worms during Pregnancy

Shortly before or at the commencement of her season the bitch due to be mated should be treated for worms. Although most adult dogs do not show signs of roundworms, a survey of 1,000 suburban dogs showed approximately 10% to be infected. Roundworms are the most important endoparasites in the puppy and the immature or larval stages of the roundworm Toxocara canis or Toxocaris leonina can pass across the placenta and infect the puppy before it is born. It is therefore essential to ensure as far as possible that the bitch is free from worms before she is mated. Although there are many preparations on general sale that are perfectly safe and effective it is worthwhile consulting your veterinary surgeon regarding worming since he will prescribe products that can be used during pregnancy when larval roundworms encysted in the body start to develop under the influence of hormonal changes. Your veterinary surgeon can also prescribe broad spectrum wormers that are perfectly safe in the pregnant animal and effectively eradicate not only roundworms but tapeworms, hookworms and whipworms if present.

3

Infertility

It is often believed that infertility among pure-bred dogs is high, and there is no doubt that many matings are unfruitful. This state of things is contrasted with the undoubted fertility of our mongrel population. The assumption is made that pedigree dogs, by reason of their breeding, tend to be less fertile than those of no particular ancestry. It is hoped to show that this assumption, as it stands, is incorrect.

It must be remembered that mongrel bitches roam the streets in season and out of season, in every sense of the word. They are mated repeatedly during their heats, and it would be strange if one of many services was not successful.

Pure-bred bitches, on the other hand, are carefully guarded during their seasons, and are mated only at the time which their owners suppose to be favourable. This may in fact not be the case, and many bitches are condemned as non-breeders through their owners' lack of knowledge.

Most mongrels possess two advantages. These are freedom and exercise, about the only amenities with which the average street dog is liberally supplied. Far too many pure-bred dogs suffer from the lack of these two. With the mass production prevalent in some of our so-called 'popular' breeds a great number of dogs are condemned to the life of the concentration camp, and lead a bored, idle existence which cannot contribute in any way either to their general well-being or to their reproductive powers.

Infertility may be due to a defect in sire or dam; it may be due to bad management in many directions; it may be absolute or relative. Among its common causes the following may be mentioned:

Age

Extremes of age of either parent in either direction are likely to reduce fertility. Although in theory either dog or bitch may be capable of reproduction to the end of its life, in later years fertility tends to become less, a general decline in the reproductive function being natural, accompanying the decline of all the powers incidental to increasing age. The spermatozoa of the dog may be reduced in number or motility, and the ova of the bitch may fail to be shed, or may be unfertilizable.

There is likely to be a deterioration in the constitution of the puppies of old parents. For strong, vigorous puppies it is wise that the breeding stock should be in the prime of life, neither immature nor aged.

No young dog should be used regularly at stud at too early an age. It is a good plan to let him mate one bitch at about the age of a year, and use him perhaps a few times during his second year, but regular stud work should not be undertaken before the age of about two years.

At what age should the bitch be mated for the first time? It is a safe rule, with certain exceptions, not to mate her at her first heat, if this should occur before she is a year old. During the first twelve months of her life the bitch has to grow and mature, and make up her own frame. She is in fact a puppy, and the strain of carrying and feeding a litter can only be undertaken at the expense of her own development. Such an early pregnancy can delay maturity and 'bodying-up' of the bitch and also is unlikely to result in outstanding puppies.

There are exceptions to this rule. In certain of the large-headed breeds and toys it is usual to mate at the first heat, because the disproportionate size of the head and shoulders is said to render birth difficult when the pelvic joints are set. A litter while the bones are still soft is said to result in a permanent widening of the passage which makes future labours easier. Whether it is desirable to evolve heads so large as to interfere with the normal processes of birth is another matter. Much that has been brought about by show fashions in many breeds may seem foolish and cruel to thoughtful people.

It is unwise to put off the first litter too long. Many bitches of four or five produce their first puppies easily and successfully but there is always a risk both that mating may be more difficult and less likely to be successful, and that whelping complications may ensue. Roughly speaking, the period during which a bitch is likely to breed easily and successfully is from the age of about eighteen months to six or seven years.

To sum up: the most fruitful age for breeding stock is that at which it has reached full maturity but has not yet begun to decline in vigour.

It should hardly be necessary to point out the unwisdom of mating a bitch regularly at every heat. This is the mark of the puppy-factory owner. The analogy of wild animals which breed at every heat is a false one. It is used to justify twice-yearly matings, and also to justify the practice of mating a bitch at her first heat. In the natural state bitches come in season later, and have only one heat in the year. By domestication we have altered this rhythm of Nature, but no bitch can maintain health and vigour if used as a breeding machine, and the constitution of her puppies is likely to suffer from such a proceeding.

Over-use at Stud

The over-use at stud of a fashionable sire is undoubtedly the cause of many bitches missing to him, and as long as breeders flock to such sires and their owners are unwilling to refuse a service (and, incidentally, a stud fee) this is likely to continue. Nothing is more easily gained than a reputation for infertility, and once gained a stud dog's career is to all intents and purposes finished.

Incorrect Time of Mating

This is a common cause of failure, either to achieve mating or, having done so, to produce a litter. Leaving aside the numbers of people who embark on dog breeding without the slightest knowledge of the bitch's breeding cycle, there are too many even experienced breeders with fixed ideas of the correct day for mating. There is no fixed date for any breed or any individual member of a breed. It does not follow, either, that because a bitch has been successfully mated on any particular day that this day will be correct for her next mating.

When we realize that conception depends on the ova being shed, and ready to meet the ascending sperms, it will be clear that there is no mathematical certainty as to the day of the heat on which this will occur. There is a probability, but only this, and the correct day for mating is that on which the bitch shows her readiness for it, and not before. Far more bitches are mated too early than too late. The period during the second week of her heat usually covers the time during which a bitch will accept the dog, and in most breeds this will mean some time between the ninth and fifteenth day, largely depending on the breed. The time of acceptance usually lasts for several days, though exceptionally it may be as short as a few hours. This, however, is most unusual, and in practice the most favourable time should be twenty-four hours or so after the bitch appears perfectly ready.

When she is ready for mating she will indicate this in no uncertain manner. In the first place, the red discharge should be disappearing though there are many exceptions to this rule and it cannot be taken as a certain indication. The vagina should be softening and becoming flaccid, and this is an important sign. During the early stages of the heat the vulval orifice is swollen and hard, and in this state mating is impossible. Her behaviour also shows plainly that the bitch is ready. After a preliminary stage of playfulness and coyness, she should stand rigidly, tail held aside and hindquarters braced. It is useful to test her reactions with another bitch, for a bitch ready for mating will stand as readily to another bitch as to a dog when stimulated by sniffing or licking, or even without any attentions at all. A normal bitch who tucks herself in, or persists in sitting down once the initial shyness is over, is not ready for mating. It should be noted that this applies to normal bitches, not to the naturally frigid or difficult. Should a normal bitch be forcibly mated before or after she is ready, a litter is unlikely, for conception does not depend on the act of mating but on the readiness for union of the two sets of reproductive cells.

Mating at too early a stage of the heat is one of the most usual causes of unfruitful unions. Similarly mating too late is likely to produce the same result.

Frigidity

So far we have been considering causes which may lead to infertility in animals which are normal both in health and temperament— that is to say, animals in which external circumstances are responsible for failure to get stock.

There are, however, certain dogs which for no apparent reason are extremely difficult to mate owing to frigidity. This term is usually applied to bitches, though males may also show a lack of normal sexual instinct. Apart from abormalities of structure, ill-health or obesity, this is probably due to abnormalities of the glands of internal secretion.

It is likely that frigidity in bitches may have a similar origin in the lack of balance between the secretions of the various glands governing sexual development and behaviour. Whatever the cause, the condition is a troublesome one, and such bitches may be extremely difficult or even impossible to mate. In these cases the proper time for mating cannot be estimated as in the case of normal bitches, and a suggested remedy is to keep dog and bitch together during the entire time of probable acceptance, attempting to mate them every day.

Forcible mating is comparatively easy in small breeds as two people can control a small bitch fairly easily. In larger breeds it is difficult. The actions of a bitch in resisting mating are likely to be violent and in large, strong bitches almost impossible to control. Three people are not too many to manage the bitch. One should take charge of the head, using tape or a muzzle if necessary. The other two must keep the hindquarters in such a position that the dog can have access. The natural tendency of a bitch resisting mating is to sit down. This must be prevented by knees or arms under the bitch from both sides. In bitches of suitable size a knee immediately in front of both hind legs and pressing backwards will prevent the bending of the stifle joint, which must take place for the bitch to be able to sit. A hand under the vagina, from between the legs, will help to make it prominent. A good deal of strength has to be exerted to hold a strong bitch in the proper position against her will, and in spite of all efforts it may be impossible to do so, especially if the bitch tries to throw herself down bodily, which she may easily do. It may happen that once the tie has been effected the bitch may stand quietly, but if she does not, restraint will have to be maintained throughout the entire period of possibly half an hour or longer, for if relaxed the dog may be injured by the bitch's violence. Many stud dogs, used to normal natural matings, may refuse to mate a bitch in such abnormal conditions.

It is doubtful, in my opinion, whether it is worth while or even wise to mate such bitches. They may pass on the peculiarity to their offspring, and in any case are a doubtful proposition as regards progeny.

Improper Feeding

In addition to other factors, fertility depends on a balanced diet containing adequate supplies of all the necessary elements. In the case of the dog, this includes a proper supply of meat; an excess of starch cannot make up for deficiencies in this respect. The vitamin content of the diet is most important.

Successful pregnancy and the rearing of healthy litters depends on a proper supply of vitamins, especially Vitamins A and D, concerned with growth and the resistance to infection. When the dam is lacking in these the development and stamina of the progeny will be affected. During the weeks of intra-uterine development, and throughout the period of suckling, the puppies can receive supplies only from the blood of the dam, and later from her milk, and these supplies will depend on her own diet.

Various minerals are also essential for health, growth and reproductive powers. These include iron, calcium, phosphorus, salt, iodine and so on, and also the rarer minerals, of which only traces are needed, such as cobalt and manganese. The calcium-phosphorus balance of the body is of prime importance, not only because, activated by Vitamin D, it is needed for growth and bone development, but also because it has been found, by research among cattle, to be vital for the conception rate. Animals which lack an adequate supply of well-balanced calcium and phosphorus have a much lower rate of conception than those which have ample supplies. Vitamin D is needed for the absorption and utilization of these two minerals, and where it is absent we find weakness and deformity of the skeleton, commonly seen in rickets.

Mention of these important factors in diet should not create the impression that the chemist's shop is their only source. An ample, well-balanced diet will contain most, if not all, the essential vitamins, though supplements may be needed. Vitamins A and D in the form of cod-liver or halibut-liver oil, and the Vitamin B complex in the form of brewer's yeast, of which Vetzyme is a good preparation, can be used with advantage throughout the year while additional calcium and phosphorus in one of their many prepared forms is advisable for puppies, and for brood bitches throughout their breeding lives.

The ideal diet for a dog should consist of a balanced diet with approximately 10–20% protein and at least 3% fat which is the natural energy source for the dog. On a dry matter basis this is not less than 25% protein and about 10% fat. Carbohydrate (starch) offers a cheaper alternative energy source but the feeding of excess biscuits leads to loss of condition and obesity. A balanced diet can be easily and cheaply provided using any of the reputable commercial diets, canned, semi-moist or dry, provided manufacturers' instructions are rigorously adhered to. Alternatively, home prepared diets with meat, milk and good quality biscuit plus an additional source of essential fatty acids and amino acids in the form of liver, eggs etc. can be prepared, although such diets are more time-consuming and costly and are unlikely to be superior.

Lack of Exercise

It may seem strange to list this as a cause of lack of fertility. Nevertheless it may be an important contributory factor, and we have only to realize the failure to breed shown by wild animals in a state of close captivity to see that it may well be so.

If one were asked what was the greatest defect of many big kennels today, the answer would be lack of exercise. Many breeders keep far more dogs than they can exercise properly, especially in these days of limited help. Many dogs spend their entire lives cooped up in small kennels, with perhaps a few minutes' freedom in yard or paddock daily. How can this state of affairs be anything but detrimental to an active, freedom-loving animal like the dog? The result is poor muscular development, not only of the muscles of the skeleton but also of important internal muscles, those of the heart, and bowel, and other organs, including the uterus. This leads to sluggish circulation, constipation and a general slowing down of all bodily functions, including those of reproduction.

Investigation among farm animals has shown that bulls given regular daily exercise are more fertile than those which are closely confined. There is little doubt that the same must apply to dogs.

Abrnomalities of Health or Structure

Hormone Deficiencies

Hormones, as we shall see in a later chapter, are chemical messengers, secreted by various important glands, called endocrine glands. The hormone secretions pass direct into the blood stream, and exercise their effect in the various parts of the body, carried there by the circulation of the blood.

The balance between these glands is delicate; the effect of their secretions may be additive or opposing, and if one or more fail to function satisfactorily, the whole team, for such it is, is thrown out of gear with far-reaching effects to the body in general and the reproductive system in particular.

Local Malformations and Diseases

Such conditions are common causes of breeding failures. Infections of the uterus, tubes or ovaries of the bitch; a stricture of the vagina, or the presence of an obstructing tumour, or a so-called prolapse, are not uncommon.

Infections of the Uterus and its Appendages

Metritis, an infection of the mucous lining of the uterus can occur, particularly after a difficult whelping. Bruising, trauma and secondary bacterial infection are the usual causes.

The symptoms vary according to the severity of the infection; acute cases may linger on to become chronic, or pus may develop in the uterus, giving rise to enlargement, pain, fever and all the accompaniments of acute infection.

Metritis is occasionally met with in maiden bitches, lowering resistance due to cold or chilling may be predisposing factors allowing germs already present to multiply. Veterinary treatment involving modern antibiotics usually clears the trouble up without complications. The modern sulpha drugs and penicillin, with other similar preparations, should, if correctly used early in the disease, rob it of many of its terrors, but any chronically diseased condition of the uterus and its lining must obviously be a deterrent to conception.

Chronic metritis usually causes irregular bleeding, and sometimes a discharge and can be mistaken for true heat. The disease should be suspected if bleeding occurs often and at irregular intervals. Veterinary advice should be sought if you are in any doubt.

Strictures

These contractions of the vagina are occasionally met with; they offer a mechanical hindrance to mating, and in any case in which the dog is unable to effect penetration the vagina should be examined, and if necessary dilated by a veterinary surgeon.

Tumours of the Vagina

Various forms of tumour occur in the vagina, both malignant growths and comparatively harmless swellings, mainly of a fibrous nature. These also may present an obstruction to the dog, and should always be examined by a veterinary surgeon. Under this heading must be included the so-called prolapse of the vagina.

Prolapse of the Vagina

This condition has sometimes been called a vaginal hernia. It is neither a prolapse in the correct sense of the word, nor a hernia. It is a temporary overgrowth of the vaginal lining (mucus membrane), at the active stage of the reproductive cycle which occurs during heat. It appears to be due to over-activity of one of the ovarian hormones, oestrogen, which stimulates the lining of the uterus to receive the fertilized egg. The usual sequence of events is that, at the first heat, the vagina is more swollen and prominent than normal, and after a few days a rounded dark swelling appears at the vulva. In mild cases the swelling will not be extruded, but it may become larger and protrude outside the vagina. It is actually part of the lining membrane which has enlarged. Veterinary advice should be sought, particularly if breeding is intended. Often the condition will not recur at subsequent heats if early treatment is instituted.

Contracted Pelvis

Mainly as a result of rickets, the pelvic bones may become deformed, narrowing the bony outlet and, when the deformity is severe, presenting an insuperable obstacle to parturition. In such cases a Caesarian operation offers the most likely chance of a living litter, and humanity suggests that such a bitch should not be bred from again. In some breeds, owing to the dictates of show fashions, such abnormally large heads and shoulders have been evolved that their passage through even a normal pelvis is difficult or impossible. It is hard to speak calmly of such folly. Difficulties and mishaps occur often enough without deliberately inviting them.

So far we have been concerned only with the bitch. The dog also suffers from disabilities of structure which may interfere with his capacity for mating.

Phimosis

This is the rare condition in which the sheath of the penis is so tight that it cannot be retracted. The simple operation of circumcision will correct this.

Non-descent of the Testicles

The normal position of these organs during intra-uterine life is within the abdomen. They begin to descend through the inguinal canal shortly before birth, usually reaching the scrotum at birth or shortly after. Instead of descending normally, one or both testicles may be retained within the abdomen, either high, near the kidney where they started or at any lower point.

Cryptorchidism

The name given to the condition in which one or both testicles are absent from the scrotum. If one testicle only is retained, the dog is described as a unilateral cryptorchid, if both are absent it is a bilateral cryptorchid.

The older term, still often used, of monorchid for a dog with only one testicle to be seen, is anatomically incorrect, it should be used only in cases of dogs possessing only one testicle, and not merely a hidden one.

Bilateral cryptorchids are sterile, the sperms which normally develop at sexual maturity fail to do so in a retained testicle, the raised temperature within the body compared with that in the scrotum being concerned with lack of development.

Sexual instincts are unimpaired, even in the bilateral cryptorchid, for they are controlled by the internal secretions of the testicle called androgens. Unilateral cryptorchids are fertile, for, though fewer sperms than normal are produced, they are still vastly more numerous than the eggs to be fertilized. Some of this class, however, do seem to have their fertility impaired and are not very successful sires.

The general opinion among veterinary surgeons, geneticists and large numbers of experienced breeders is that the condition, as usually met with, is inherited, and is due to a simple Mendelian recessive gene. A good deal of opposition, not always well informed and unprejudiced, exists among breeders. A better understanding of the rudiments of genetics will show that inheritance of this kind is not incompatible with absence of any signs of the defect, even in a number of generations of offspring of an affected sire. One of the hormones of the anterior pituitary gland controls the descent of the testicles, and hormones are produced and controlled by the actions of hereditary factors called genes. Thus the link with heredity is not difficult to establish.

Kennel Club breed standards state 'Male animals should have two apparently normal testicles fully descended into the scrotum.' Dogs which are not entire are judged as deviating from the normal and should be penalized by judges in exactly the same way as they would penalize any other fault.

Among other physical disabilities is that of failure to tie the bitch, though many fruitful matings have been effected without the tie, which is brought about by means of a bulb of erectile tissue at the base of the penis. This becomes engorged during sexual excitement and swells in such a way as to maintain unbreakable contact with the female for a period varying from a few minutes to half an hour or even longer in individual cases. The seminal fluid is expelled during this time and, owing to the tie, cannot escape but is forced into the uterus and uterine horns where the eggs are waiting to be fertilized.

There may be loss of sexual power in the dog, owing to malnutrition, exhaustion, disease or old age, and, owing no doubt to a hormone deficiency, there are dogs which either show no inclination to mate throughout their lives or, while displaying normal sexual excitement, can never be brought to the act of mating.

We have also occasionally to deal with personal idiosyncrasies on the part of both dog and bitch, who may steadily refuse to take any interest in one partner, though quite willing to mate with another. It should always be remembered that dogs are not mere breeding machines; they have personalities and characters of their own, as individuals, and these should be respected. Many pedigree matings today take on certain aspects reminiscent of rape.

Infections influencing Fertility

There are today many bacteria and also some viruses that can influence fertility. Betahaemolytic streptococcus (BHS) has long been implicated in this respect. E. coli – coliforms, and a variety of viruses can also be involved. To date however there has been no evidence that canine parvovirus disease can affect fertility, despite the claims of some breeders. Not only can these various organisms, bacterial and viral, cause infertility problems but also they are implicated in neonatal death or the 'fading puppy' syndrome. Swabs do help to type the organisms but these have to be taken at the correct time and carefully preserved if they are to be of any value in analysis. The matter should be discussed with your veterinary surgeon.

So-called 'Vaginal Acidity' of the Bitch

This condition is popularly credited with failure to conceive, since acidity kills the sperm cells. How far there is any proof that failure of conception is due to this cause may be open to doubt, although it finds a place in much of the literature on dogs. It may well be that, like so many other theories, it is copied from one book to another without any real testing of validity.

The normal vaginal secretion is slightly acid. On the face of it, it would seem strange that Nature, with her insistence on the continuation of the species, should fail in this important respect. In fact, the preliminary fluid ejected by the dog in the act of mating, that from the prostatic gland, is itself alkaline and should provide against any undue acidity of the bitch, ensuring that the sperm cells, ejected later, should be received into a suitable medium. Those who hold this theory of acidity advise a mild alkaline douche before mating. Acidity is tested by means of blue litmus paper, which turns red on contact with acid.

When the many likely causes of infertility have been investigated, including an examination for living sperms in the semen if necessary, there will always be a small percentage of dogs which are non-breeders or unreliable breeders, owing, probably, to some fault in the genetic make-up of the reproductive system of the individual concerned.

4

Whelping

Some form of bed or box is needed. A well-lined basket is suitable for toy breeds, but on the whole a wooden box is better for the larger breeds, and a big strong packing case can be used. In any whelping box there must be room for the bitch to lie comfortably with plenty of space for the litter, for the box can be used for both as long as the puppies are in the nest.

A packing case should lie on its side with a ledge fixed to retain the bedding. The open box has many advantages when whelping quarters are heated. Removable floorboards which can be taken out for scrubbing keep the nest beautifully clean, and a movable ledge in front makes it easy to keep puppies in or to let them out.

During whelping, and for a day or two afterwards, a movable rail, similar to the pig rail of the farmer, can be fitted about three inches or so from the floor round the three sides of the box.

This will prevent newly born puppies from being crushed against the sides of the box by a clumsy or careless bitch. After a couple of days the whelps are active enough to get out of her way, and the rail can be removed.

Most bitches are clever with their litters, and contrive to get into a box full of puppies, shuffle them out of the middle and lie down among them in the neatest possible way, or to change their position by the same method, but the occasional careless or clumsy bitch will be found, and the rail may prevent the loss of a puppy.

Supervision

The amount of supervision will depend largely on the temperament of the bitch, and perhaps too on that of her owner.

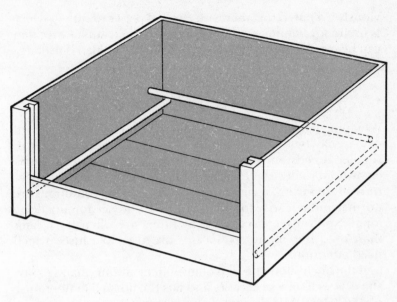

WHELPING BOX

A guard rail is figured at the back of the box. Similar rails may
be fixed at each side if it is considered necessary. Only one of
the two longitudinal sections in the front of the box is shown

Fussiness and agitation are out of place, but quiet supervision
of some sort there must be, or the bitches may have to endure
unnecessary suffering and puppies may be lost.

The owner who has the confidence and affection of the
bitch will be welcome, perhaps even essential, for some
bitches will not settle down to the job alone. In every case a
close eye must be kept on the progress of whelping, especially
in a maiden bitch, once she has started to strain. It is only by
such supervision that the owner becomes aware in time that all
is not going normally. The safest plan is to remain with the
bitch from the time she starts to strain until the last whelp is
born, though this may be a counsel of perfection for the last
puppy may be born some time after the others.

Preparations for whelping should be made in good time.
Plenty of clean newspapers, rough warm towels, cotton wool
and a mild antiseptic such as Dettol or Savlon should be pre-

viously prepared together with a roll of paper towelling which is useful for helping puppies out that are in trouble since they can be very slippery. A ball pen or fibre tipped pen is useful as a means of identifying any particular puppy.

Signs of Approaching Labour

Whelping usually occurs about the sixty-second or sixty-third day, it may be earlier in big breeds with large litters, later in smaller breeds and with small litters. Delays beyond forty-eight hours after the expected date are common, but there must always exist an element of doubt whether conditions are normal and it is wise to call in veterinary advice for any delay longer than three days. Healthy litters are often born later than this, but many such cases are due to causes which need attention.

If the bitch shows no sign of imminent labour, that is to say, she eats well, takes exercise, and has the normal temperature of 38.5°C. (101.4°F.), and if the owner can feel the puppies move, then there is no need for alarm. If her temperature has dropped two degrees or so, and if in addition she is having periods of restlessness with apparent discomfort and occasional straining, but these subside without any sequel, then it is essential to have expert advice. Such conditions may be due to uterine inertia, to be mentioned later in this chapter.

The normal signs of approaching labour are often unmistakable. For a day or two before whelping the bitch may be disinclined for exercise, but this does not always happen, and bitches can go off on a hunting expedition, or exercising with horses, and come home afterwards to have a quick and easy whelping completed within a few hours.

Hands may be upheld in horror at such an idea; the writer can ony say that the Victorian idea of the lady in 'an interesting condition' appears to exist still in matters concerning the bitch in whelp, and the equivalent of the sofa is still often insisted on, with detriment, in the writer's opinion, to the muscles of the bitch which are needed in parturition and also to her general health.

The first sign that whelping is imminent is the desire to make a nest, and the bitch should be accustomed to her whelping quarters in advance and given some old material which she can tear up, otherwise she may make her own selection. The writer can speak with feeling on this point.

Newspaper is a very useful bedding material for the whelping bitch particularly in the house. Several layers are needed and these can be removed when soiled. The newspapers can be covered with one of the acrylic fur fabrics, Vet Bed or similar which can easily be washed. Have at least one replacement to substitute as necessary.

Some hours before labour starts, the vagina begins to soften and pout, and a sticky discharge is noticed. A fall in temperature is the most certain sign of approaching labour and it usually occurs several days before whelping, the drop being from the normal of 38.5°C. (101.4°F.) to about 37.2°C. (99°F.).

One can say safely that a bitch whose temperature is normal is not likely to whelp for at least twenty-four hours. The fall is doubtless a natural method of preparing the whelps for the change in temperature which occurs at birth, and which, even with artificial heat provided, is still considerable.

It should be mentioned that signs may occasionally be slight, and go unnoticed by the unobservant owner.

Normal Whelping

Whelping is, or should be, a natural and normal process, and in a healthy well-formed bitch, mated to a dog of appropriate size, this is usually the case. In certain breeds, however, where fashion has decreed that disproportionately large heads and shoulders are desirable there may be considerable disparity between the size of the foetal head and thorax and that of the bitch's pelvis, causing great difficulty at birth. In breeds of this type complications are normal, in fact abnormal whelping has become the normal, and it is difficult to understand how the welfare of a breed and the suffering involved can be subordinated to such an artificial fashion.

Difficulties and abnormalities will be described later, and a description of the normal mechanism of birth will show what is to be expected.

At the end of the period of gestation, that is about the sixty-

Table showing when a bitch is due to whelp

Served January.	Due to Whelp March.	Served February.	Due to Whelp April.	Served March.	Due to Whelp May.	Served April.	Due to Whelp June.	Served May.	Due to Whelp July.	Served June.	Due to Whelp August.	Served July.	Due to Whelp September.	Served August.	Due to Whelp October.	Served September.	Due to Whelp November.	Served October.	Due to Whelp December.	Served November.	Due to Whelp January.	Served December.	Due to Whelp February.
1	5	1	5	1	3	1	3	1	3	1	3	1	2	1	3	1	3	1	3	1	3	1	2
2	6	2	6	2	4	2	4	2	4	2	4	2	3	2	4	2	4	2	4	2	4	2	3
3	7	3	7	3	5	3	5	3	5	3	5	3	3	3	5	3	5	3	5	3	5	3	4
4	8	4	8	4	6	4	6	4	6	4	6	4	4	4	6	4	6	4	6	4	6	4	5
5	9	5	9	5	7	5	7	5	7	5	7	5	6	5	7	5	7	5	7	5	7	5	6
6	10	6	10	6	8	6	8	6	8	6	8	6	7	6	8	6	8	6	8	6	8	6	7
7	11	7	11	7	9	7	9	7	9	7	9	7	8	7	9	7	9	7	9	7	9	7	8
8	12	8	12	8	10	8	10	8	10	8	10	8	9	8	10	8	10	8	10	8	10	8	9
9	13	9	13	9	11	9	11	9	11	9	11	9	10	9	11	9	11	9	11	9	11	9	10
10	14	10	14	10	12	10	12	10	12	10	12	10	11	10	12	10	12	10	12	10	12	10	11
11	15	11	15	11	13	11	13	11	13	11	13	11	12	11	13	11	13	11	13	11	13	11	12
12	16	12	16	12	14	12	14	12	14	12	14	12	13	12	14	12	14	12	14	12	14	12	13
13	17	13	17	13	15	13	15	13	15	13	15	13	14	13	15	13	15	13	15	13	15	13	14
14	18	14	18	14	16	14	16	14	16	14	16	14	15	14	16	14	16	14	16	14	16	14	15
15	19	15	19	15	17	15	17	15	17	15	17	15	16	15	17	15	17	15	17	15	17	15	16
16	20	16	20	16	18	16	18	16	18	16	18	16	17	16	18	16	18	16	18	16	18	16	17
17	21	17	21	17	19	17	19	17	19	17	19	17	18	17	19	17	19	17	19	17	19	17	18
18	22	18	22	18	20	18	20	18	20	18	20	18	19	18	20	18	20	18	20	18	20	18	19
19	23	19	23	19	21	19	21	19	21	19	21	19	20	19	21	19	21	19	21	19	21	19	20
20	24	20	24	20	22	20	22	20	22	20	22	20	21	20	22	20	22	20	22	20	22	20	21
21	25	21	25	21	23	21	23	21	23	21	23	21	22	21	23	21	23	21	23	21	23	21	22
22	26	22	26	22	24	22	24	22	24	22	24	22	23	22	24	22	24	22	24	22	24	22	23
23	27	23	27	23	25	23	25	23	25	23	25	23	24	23	25	23	25	23	25	23	25	23	24
24	28	24	28	24	26	24	26	24	26	24	26	24	25	24	26	24	26	24	26	24	26	24	25
25	29	25	29	25	27	25	27	25	27	25	27	25	26	25	27	25	27	25	27	25	27	25	26
26	30	26	30	26	28	26	28	26	28	26	28	26	27	26	28	26	28	26	28	26	28	26	27
27	31	27	1 (MAY)	27	29	27	29	27	29	27	29	27	28	27	29	27	29	27	29	27	29	27	28
28	1 (APR.)	28	2	28	30	28	30	28	30	28	30	28	29	28	30	28	30	28	30	28	30	28	1 (MAR.)
29	2	29	3	29	31	29	1 (JULY)	29	31	29	31	29	30	29	31	29	1 (DEC.)	29	31	29	31	29	2
30	3			30	1 (JUNE)	30	2	30	1 (AUG.)	30	1 (SEP.)	30	1 (OCT.)	30	1 (NOV.)	30	2	30	1 (JAN.)	30	1 (FEB.)	30	3
31	4			31	2			31	2			31	2	31	2			31	2			31	4

second or sixty-third day, when the whelps are sufficiently developed to begin an independent existence, a train of physiological events is set in motion by the reproductive hormones which results in their expulsion from the uterus.

Each puppy is attached throughout gestation to the uterine horn by means of the placenta or afterbirth, the umbilical cord connecting puppy and placenta. This attachment enables the maternal blood to communicate with the foetal circulation providing all the nourishment and the oxygen needed by the growing embryo through the blood vessels of the cord, and carrying away the waste products in exchange. The placenta, cord and whelp are enclosed in a membranous sac and are self-contained, except in the uncommon event of true twins, which share a single placenta.

This sac, the bag of membranes as it is called, contains fluid which not only acts as a dilating agent in the passage through the birth canal, but also forms a cushion to protect the puppy within it from pressure damage during birth.

The process of labour is divided into two stages, excluding the final stage of the return of the system to normal.

Stage One. Approaching birth is initiated by irregular and spasmodic contractions of the uterine muscle. These are not the powerful rhythmical contractions of the later stage, and they are not perceptible to the eye, nor to a hand laid on the abdomen. They bring about the relaxation and dilation of the lower parts of the birth passages, the uterine body, vagina and vulva. They appear to be slightly painful, and cause restlessness and discomfort. The genital passages enlarge and soften during this stage, and secrete quantities of mucus which acts as a lubricant for the passage of the whelps. This process continues until the parts are completely softened and expanded. It is only when this point has been reached that the whelps can be born.

The time taken varies within fairly wide limits; it may last a few hours; it may be prolonged for a day or even longer. No attempt should be made to shorten it. The surrounding fluid which dilates the parts also cushions the puppies against pressure, and no anxiety for them or the bitch need be felt, for the contractions are not powerful or regular, and are not exhausting to her or damaging to the puppies.

Stage Two.   The second stage of labour begins as soon as the genital passages are dilated as the result of the first stage. At this point the picture changes, and there is no difficulty in deciding when stage two has supervened. Contractions which before were imperceptible and irregular now become rhythmical and powerful. They can be both seen and felt in the balling and hardening of the uterus, which is noticeable to a hand laid on the bitch's abdomen. This hardening occurs during the contraction, which may last a few seconds. When it is over, the uterus relaxes and the bitch pants. Panting, indeed, may be the first thing to be noticed if the bitch is not being closely observed. It indicates the approaching birth of the first puppy.

A series of these powerful contractions gradually force the lowest lying puppy through the passages. It is usually preceded by the bag of membranes, which appears as a rounded swelling at the vulva. The bag will appear at the height of a contraction, and will probably disappear once or twice as the uterus relaxes, but it will reappear and finally burst, releasing the fluid it contains. Membranes may not break until after the head is born, if so they must be broken in order that the puppy may breathe. The natural rupture of the bag of membranes usually heralds the birth of the first puppy, normally born head first with the forepaws alongside the nose or on the chest. A maiden bitch often suffers pain at the birth of the first puppy, and may cry out. After the head is born there will be a slight pause, and the shoulders will emerge with the next contraction. The smaller hindquarters usually slip out easily.

It is quite usual for puppies to be born rump first; this is called a breech presentation. The hindlegs are forward on either side of the body. Breech presentation sometimes causes problems due to the width of the pelvis. Do not delay. Seek veterinary advice since if the puppy is not born fairly quickly it will die. The blood supply is cut off in the birth canal and since it will be unable to breathe as the head is the last part to be born rapid delivery is essential. Another backward presentation is the so-called posterior presentation where the hindlegs are presented and are followed by the rump. This usually presents little problem and can almost be regarded as normal in the bitch. Here again birth must be fairly rapid in order that suffocation does not occur once the placental blood supply has been cut off as the puppy passes through the pelvis. Gentle traction on the puppy may be necessary in order to ensure that the head is born without delay.

A further contraction should produce the placenta, which the mother will proceed to eat, dividing the cord with her teeth close to the navel of the puppy as soon as she has swallowed the rest.

Each puppy is normally born in its own bag of membranes, though this may be broken during birth. If the membranes are still intact, the bitch will bite them through immediately the puppy is born. If she does not, or cannot do so owing to an undershot jaw, the puppy must be released at once. This is easily managed by a finger, breaking the film at the pup's mouth, which will enable it to breathe and expand its lungs for the first time.

Unborn whelps do not breathe, they receive the necessary oxygen from the blood of the dam, by means of the placenta. Once this has separated from the uterine wall, the supply of oxygen is abruptly cut off, and can henceforth only be obtained by means of the puppy's own breathing. Once the placenta has separated, therefore, the puppy must breathe or die.

It is not unusual for a maiden bitch to be a little bewildered at the strange things which are happening to her, and she may not attempt to bite through the cord of the first puppy. In this case, after waiting half a minute or so to enable as much blood as possible to enter the puppy's circulation from the cord, this should be gently squeezed flat between finger and thumb, pressing the blood towards the puppy, and then cut with sterilized scissors about half an inch from the navel. This will also obviate the need to tie the cord, though this can be done with sterilized thread if necessary. The bitch will then proceed to lick the puppy dry, licking serving also to stimulate it by the massage of her tongue, and by the time this is done, the next will probably be on the way. It is almost normal for membranes to be broken before the whelp emerges, and the placenta also occasionally separates before birth. This is most likely to happen in the later stages of a large litter when the uterine muscle is tiring. And so, although a contraction has dislodged the placenta, there may be delay before the next contraction expels the puppy. During this time it is in danger of drowning, its oxygen supply through the placenta is cut off, and it cannot yet breathe. It may gasp and draw fluid into its lungs. If, therefore, any part of a puppy appears once or twice without its membranes, and is stained and discoloured with blood, it is a good thing to ease it out if possible, as described shortly.

The interval between births is variable, in many cases fifteen to thirty minutes elapse between the birth of each whelp, but it is quite usual for several to be born on each others' heels, and then for a long gap to occur. Towards the end of a large litter (and twelve to fourteen puppies are not unusual in some breeds) several hours, even half a day, may elapse, during which time the uterus rests and recovers its tone before contracting once more to expel the rest of the litter.

Such a resting time is beneficial, and if the bitch is resting quietly and comfortably without straining or panting, the delay need cause no anxiety. The delay caused by any obstruction has quite a different character.

The second stage of birth is usually completed in comparatively few hours, perhaps six to ten or so. There is normally no serious delay. If, instead of resting, the bitch is clearly trying hard to get rid of a puppy without success, the situation calls for expert help, for the powerful contractions of the second stage of labour are exhausting to the bitch and dangerous to the puppies if they are prolonged.

It is not easy to be sure when the last puppy has been born, but with the uterus relaxed, as it is immediately after the birth of several puppies, it may be possible to feel the outlines of one left in the uterus, which begins to contract down when the last whelp has been expelled, though it naturally does not return to its normal state for a period.

During whelping the bitch will probably be glad of a drink of warm milk and glucose, and this may be repeated as often as she will take it. Most healthy normal bitches come through their ordeal in good shape, and healthy litters are contented and quiet from the moment of birth. They begin to suckle immediately, and the writer has seen puppies attach themselves to a nipple and start sucking vigorously before their hindquarters have even emerged into the outside world.

Should the newly born puppies be left with the bitch while the rest of the litter is born? Breeders' views differ on this point. One school thinks they should be removed to a warm and cosy box nearby, the other leaves them with the dam. It must depend on the bitch. If maternally minded she may fret and worry if they are taken away, especially if she hears them cry. If she is upset and distracted, removal may be the best course. The writer's view is that, if there is no real reason to the contrary, puppies should be left with their mother. Her constant licking and turning them about is a valuable stimulus to respiration and circulation, both newly established after birth. If the bitch ignores her whelps, or does not quite know what to do, as may happen in a first litter, the breeder must step in to take her place. A rough warm towel, in which the puppy can be wrapped and gently but firmly rubbed will meet the case, which is then best dealt with by a separate box until all the puppies are born.

The Post-Whelping Period

It will be readily understood that the genital organs take a little time to return to normal, after the weeks of pregnancy and the eventual birth of the whelps. During the first week or two, there is likely to be a good deal of blood-stained discharge, which often contains clots of blood from the placental sites in the uterus. Any serious bleeding from these points is normally controlled by the rapid contraction of the uterus when empty, but oozing may continue for some short time. The uterine discharges become greenish when exposed to the air, and many puppies are born with green stains on their coats, especially noticeable in light coat colours. These wear off fairly quickly.

The discharge of blood and mucus usually stops by the end of ten days or a fortnight. The temperature which rises a degree or two after whelping, should become normal by the end of forty-eight hours. Should it remain raised, or should the discharge become offensive or show traces of pus, it is a sign of sepsis and help should be sought at once. The modern antibiotics have revolutionized treatment in such cases, nevertheless early treatment means quicker recovery, and less interruption in the feeding routine of the whelps.

The bitch's motions will be copious and black for the first few days after whelping, especially if she has eaten a large number of placentas. They may also be frequent and loose. This is normal, and no anxiety need be felt unless the condition is prolonged. A preparation such as light kaolin powder is useful in controlling this form of diarrhoea and can be given in teaspoon doses in the food. In severe or prolonged cases, a veterinary surgeon should be consulted. It is unwise to give remedies of unknown composition in view of possible effects on the puppies.

Placenta eating by the bitch is an instinctive reaction, and there are few instinctive habits in animals which do not originate in some need of those concerned. It is known that the placenta is a temporary endocrine organ, having an internal secretion which is a powerful stimulant to milk production.

In the normal bitch the maternal instinct is strongly developed. During the first day or two she may need to be coaxed to leave her litter, even for the purpose of relieving herself, and become anxious if kept away for more than a few minutes.

She must be taken outside by a collar and lead if necessary, and can be released as soon as she has obliged. Bitches which dislike even getting out of the nest can have their food in bed if they prefer it, this stage will last only for a few days. Feeding the nursing bitch is dealt with in the chapter on puppy rearing.

Handling of puppies by the owner is another debated point, and again it must be decided by the character of the bitch. If she has complete confidence n her owner, she will probably not resent handling, especially if she is accustomed to it from birth. Beds must be made, boxes must be cleaned, dew claws removed, nails trimmed, and so on. Puppies used to gentle handling from birth are usually much easier to manage in after life. They learn quickly to trust their owner, and adapt themselves much more easily to the changes which inevitably occur when they go to a new home.

Eclampsia or Milk Fever

This is a condition due to the sudden lack of calcium in the blood due to the amount of calcium secreted in the milk. It can be sudden in onset particularly in bitches with a copious milk supply that have large litters and are extremely maternal. Usually it occurs at the height of lactation, at about the second or third week but can occur within a few days of whelping. I have also seen cases actually prior to whelping. The first thing to be noticed is a stiffness of the hindlegs and if veterinary advice is not rapidly sought the condition soon progresses to convulsions and lack of consciousness. An injection of a special calcium preparation effects a rapid recovery in the majority of cases.

Care must be taken to ensure that the bitch receives additional calcium and phosphorus during pregnancy, remembering that this can only be utilized in the presence of Vitamin D, and that the correct ratio of the two minerals is essential. Furthermore, bitches should not be asked to feed too many puppies, and the large amount of calcium passed on in their milk should be replaced by food with its necessary supplements. Eclampsia appears to be inherent in certain strains. Although calcium, phosphorus and vitamins A and D are essential supplements during pregnancy and lactation, oral administration of calcium will not always prevent eclampsia, which is due to the sudden drop in blood calcium levels, and not an overall calcium lack. Bitches with repeated attacks of eclampsia should not be bred from.

Abnormal Whelping

Certain conditions occur in which the possibility of abnormal whelping must be considered. In some cases the alarm may be false, but only the event will prove this. It is not safe to assume that, in spite of unusual circumstances, puppies will be born without risk to themselves or to their dam. Any condition involving the possibility of danger, to dam or puppies, must be considered abnormal, and precautions taken.

The following suggest themselves as conditions in which whelping may become abnormal.

1. Undue delay in the onset of labour after the expected date
2. Delay in the smooth progress from the preliminary stage of dilatation to that of expulsion.
3. Weakening or total cessation of contractions when it is obvious that there are puppies still to be born.
4. The presence of strong contractions without the birth of a puppy over anything but a fairly short period.

Whenever whelping does not seem to be progressing normally, and whenever any of the above signs are present, qualified and competent veterinary help should be sought without delay. The successful treatment of any difficulty must be preceded by accurate diagnosis of its causes, and this is the province of the veterinary surgeon. Unskilled interference may cause severe suffering to the bitch, it may result in her loss, and that of her litter. The more experienced the breeder, the more ready he is to call in skilled help, for he realizes more clearly than the novice the possibilities of disaster. Many experienced breeders have a good practical knowledge of the whelping difficulties which have come their way, and the way of their friends, but any active interference must be the responsibility of the expert. The untrained individual, even should he have considerable experience, has little knowledge of detailed anatomy, and still less of the risks of sepsis; however conversant he may be with the difficulties he has himself met, he is likely to be completely at a loss in difficulties outside his own experience, for he has no foundation of knowledge which is aware of possibilities.

Successful treatment of any serious condition needs both theoretical knowledge and experience, and a veterinary surgeon with obstetrical experience of small animals is the ideal of any breeder. The theoretical knowledge which enables him to assess possibilities must be backed up by the experience which gives operative skill. Small-animal obstetrics differ from that of the larger animals by reason of the small and restricted space involved. In the average sized bitch there is hardly room for more than two fingers in the vagina, still less if the use of any instrument is needed. To use forceps successfully, the presenting part of the puppy must be within reach of the examining finger; the forceps are passed in, guided by a finger. The operator must be certain, in this way, that when applied, they grasp the puppy, *and nothing else*. It is not rare for careless or unskilful people to rupture the uterine wall by pushing forceps through it, or to grasp part of the vagina or uterus as well as the puppy, and tear it away, with disastrous results. At full term the uterus is soft and friable, and this should never be forgotten in any manipulations.

It is hardly necessary to say how important the breeder's careful observations and notes can be on such occasions. The essence of success in any case of complicated whelping is early diagnosis and skilled treatment. Such treatment does not necessarily involve immediate interference. What used to be called, and doubtless still is, 'meddlesome midwifery', that urge to do something, instead of allowing Nature to persue her sometimes leisurely course, is as misplaced in dogs as it is in humans. The breeder often wants to hurry whelping unduly. This should never be done for the sake of convenience, or for any other reason than the interest of the bitch and her puppies. The breeder's job is to notice any signs which may be abnormal, the function of the veterinary surgeon is to interpret these signs correctly, and to act upon them according to his knowledge and skill, bearing in mind the interests of the bitch and her family as the first consideration.

Causes of Abnormal Whelping

Delay and difficulty in whelping are due to two main causes; first, the weakness or absence of normal uterine contractions which is called 'inertia'; second, some mechanical obstruction to the passage of the whelps, either foetal or maternal in origin.

Uterine Inertia is the name given to a condition in which the normal powerful uterine contractions which expel the puppies are either weak or absent. The wall of the uterus consists of thick and powerful muscle tissue, and it is muscular power, initiated by the hormones of the ductless glands, which cause the uterus to contract and thereby force the whelps through the maternal passages.

For purposes of description, inertia may be divided into two classes, primary and secondary.

Primary Uterine Inertia, a constitutional condition, due to a variety of causes. As with the external muscles of the body the internal muscular system is also impaired by age. Heart, intestine, and uterine muscles are all likely to suffer, and breeding from elderly bitches may often give rise to difficulties and to inertia. Poor condition, whether due to inadequate feeding, lack of exercise, or too-frequent pregnancies also impairs muscular efficiency, and may cause inertia, and the puppy-factory methods, which regard bitches purely as breeding machines, must result in many unfortunate bitches being worn out long before their time. Abnormalities of hormone action play a part in inertia. The activities of the reproductive system are controlled by a series of hormones as will be seen in Chapter Eleven. Hormones themselves are the result of gene action. It is thus likely that such functional abnormalities have a familial basis.

Secondary Uterine Inertia. A condition very different in cause from that just described. In both cases contractions fail to occur, but in secondary inertia this is due to the exhaustion of the uterine muscle, following excessive activity.

Thus, in an obstructed labour, after prolonged and violent contractions which fail to expel the puppy, the uterine muscle becomes exhausted and contractions cease. After a period of rest the muscle may recover its contractile power, but, in the case of an insurmountable obstacle, each succeeding period of contraction will be shorter and less effective, until all contractions finally cease, a state which may be highly dangerous to the bitch and her litter. To sum up inertia: the absence of any strong expulsive pains during labour indicates a state of primary inertia, whereas the weakening and final cessation of such pains after they had been present and normal indicates uterine exhaustion causing secondary inertia.

The strong rhythmic contractions of the expulsive stage of labour are not continuous in character; periods of rest alternate with those of activity and in every normal whelping there will be intervals, sometimes considerable, between series of contractions. Inertia need not be feared even if, for instance, a long rest takes place between the birth of two puppies. This is normal, especially towards the end of a large litter. It rests the uterine muscle and helps it to recover tone. Secondary inertia as its name implies, is caused by some outside factor, and this is usually exhaustion owing to excessive effort.

Apart from weakening the bitch, and causing delay in the birth of the puppies which may have serious effects on them, the danger of this form of inertia is uncontrolled bleeding from the uterus, which remains relaxed because it has lost the power to contract. As the puppies are born, uterine contraction stops bleeding from the placental sites. If contractile power is lost the uterus fills with blood from a number of these sites, and the outlook is extremely grave.

Secondary uterine inertia is the common result of an obstructed labour, and it is to be avoided by recognizing and dealing with the obstruction before the uterus has been seriously weakened by unsuccessful attempts to expel the puppy.

Mechanical Obstruction

Of Maternal Origin. Pelvic obstruction is the cause of many such difficulties and is often due to previously acquired pelvic injuries such as fractures sustained in road traffic accidents. If there is any history of previous injury with the bitch it is worthwhile consulting your veterinary surgeon before organising pregnancy. X-ray examination may be necessary and it is preferable to do this before she becomes pregnant. In older bitches benign tumours (polyps) sometimes occur in the genital passage and these can cause birthing difficulties.

Of Foetal Origin. Such obstructions are more common than those due to maternal causes. An abnormally large puppy cannot pass through a normal pelvis. Such large whelps, relative to the size of the bitch, may come from mating a small bitch with a large dog. Puppies may also be large because they are swollen with fluid, or are monstrosities, similar to those which occur in human obstetrics. Such freaks of nature may happen though they are rare. Since puppies are usually multiple, and may be numerous, a puppy of normal size, lying in a normal position, is not likely to give trouble. We come next to faulty positions of the whelps, which are probably the most usual cause of obstructed labour.

Malposition of Puppies

Puppies with minor degrees of malposition may be born, if not with ease, at least with no serious trouble, as in the case of a breech birth, in which the rump and tail emerge, followed by the hind legs. There are, however, some positions in which normal birth is impossible.

Should the puppy be lying transversely, that is across the pelvic inlet instead of in the long axis, head down, it cannot get into the pelvis at all. The back lies transversely across the abdomen, resting on the brim of the bony pelvis. The most violent contractions cannot overcome this obstruction.

Again, should the foetal head be bent on the chest, so that the thickness of head and thorax together must pass through the passage, ordinary birth is impossible. Some cases of malposition may be rectified by manual manipulation, and turned in such a way that delivery is possible, but not unless the puppy is within reach of the exploring finger. With modern anaesthesia Caesarian section is now as safe as and a far less traumatic procedure for the bitch than massive manipulation with its concomitant bruising. Try not to be afraid if your veterinary surgeon advises an instant Caesar.

Whatever the cause for delay or difficulty in whelping, it is not likely to be apparent to the owener; he will know either that there is delay beyond the date of whelping, or that though labour has started it is not proceeding normally and no puppies are born. Or again, that though some are born, there are clearly others to be expelled and that the bitch is unable to accomplish this.

From the practical point of view, therefore, difficult whelping can be considered under three headings:

1. Delay in the onset of labour.
2. Delay during the initial stage of labour.
3. Delay during the final stage of labour.

Delay in the Onset of Labour

Whelping dates are averages, taken over large numbers, and slight differences from such figures can be taken as normal. The gestation period usually lasts for sixty-three days, with a variation of two or three days on either side of this number. Early whelping presents no problems unless it is extremely premature, when the puppies are unlikely to survive. Delays of two or three days need not mean misfortune. On the other hand, any delays must be regarded as suggesting possibilities of trouble. It is a safe principle to secure advice if the bitch has shown no sign of starting the whelping process three or four days after the expected date. A bitch which is eating well, is lively and whose puppies are obviously alive and active is not in serious trouble at the particular moment, but should be under constant observation so that any change can be acted on at once.

Primary inertia is probably the most frequent cause of delay in the onset of whelping, a misplaced puppy can also cause delay.

Delay during the Early Stage of Labour

In cases of this kind the bitch becomes restless and uncomfortable at about the expected date. She makes her bed, and events appear to be progressing normally. Then instead of the preliminary stage passing on smoothly to the expulsive stage and the birth of puppies after a few hours, labour seems to hang fire. Discomfort passes off to a great extent, and no attempt at straining takes place. Restlessness and discomfort may recur, and pass off again, and this state may continue for several days. Although there is no urgent danger to the bitch, it should not be allowed to go on without veterinary advice. A vaginal examination will be made which will disclose whether the passage is normal and fully or partially dilated, and whether a puppy can be felt. Inertia is a probable cause of this trouble, and if conditions inside the bitch are normal, an injection of pituitrin [or the fraction of this hormone which causes contraction] will probably be given. This will cause the uterus to contract strongly, and the first puppy will be born.

In cases where the passages are normal and dilated, but no puppy can be felt by the examining finger, and where a dose of pituitrin has produced strong contractions without any advance of the first puppy, further administrations of the drug may be harmful. Other forms of treatment and primarily Caesarian section must be considered.

As mentioned earlier, Caesarian section at an early stage is far preferable before the bitch has become exhausted and repeated examinations resulted in bruising and the ever present risk of sepsis a certainty. Do not fear a routine Caesarian section!

Delay during the Final Stage of Labour

When labour has started at the expected time and when, after the preliminary stage, strong expulsive contractions have set in, the birth of the first whelp should occur within a reasonably short time, and certainly within two hours. It is often much sooner. If pains are regular and strong and still do not produce a puppy within this time there may be some obstacle to the birth. If, in particular, the first bag of membranes has appeared and broken, advice is urgently needed. When this cushioning fluid has escaped the puppy is subject to considerable pressure, and, as the water bag is normally the immediate precurser of a puppy, investigation must be made to find out the position. With the possibility of surgical measures being needed it is important, as it is in any sort of abnormal delay, that no unnecessary examinations should be made. However, provided that the hands are well scrubbed in hot soapy water and then soaked in a safe antiseptic, the owner can risk putting a finger into the vagina to see if a puppy can be felt. A swab of clean cotton wool soaked in the antiseptic should be used to clean the vaginal opening before examination. If no puppy is to be felt, veterinary advice is urgent.

Puppies cannot be removed via the normal passage if they are completely out of reach. Even forceps cannot be used successfully unless a part of the puppy can be felt to which they can be attached. Any such operations must be carried out by the veterinary surgeon and no one else.

There is urgent danger to the bitch in the unskilled use of such instruments.

The dangers of allowing the expulsive stage of labour to continue for too long are that the puppies will die from pressure, or premature separation of the placenta or that the uterine muscle will become so exhausted by fruitless contractions that it will relax completely, with haemorrhage as the result. Either condition will mean almost certain death to the bitch.

It is a safe rule to call in veterinary help if straining has been continued for two hours without any sign of a puppy. This rule applies equally to puppies born later, as to the first born. A faulty position, usually the cause, need not necessarily affect the first puppy, it may affect the last or any intervening one.

It should not however be forgotten that the uterus does not contract continuously. Work and rest alternate, and during rest, the uterine muscles recuperate. These periods may be prolonged during the birth of a large litter. A normal resting period of an hour, or even longer, is quite usual, especially towards the end. The signs of real trouble are a series of strong contractions, lasting over a period, without any result.

Positions of a puppy which are most likely to give trouble are those in which the shoulder or back is the presenting part, or in which the head is doubled down on the thorax.

Puppies lying in these positions cannot be born, and while they can sometimes be turned by a skilful veterinary surgeon, they are often too high for this to be possible. A Caesarian operation will then be the treatment of choice, and the breeder must not wait too long before seeking advice, or the favourable time will have passed, the bitch will be worn out and the genital passages infected by repeated examinations.

As an illustration of the kind of difficulties which may be encountered, the writer gives details of two cases which occurred in her own bitches, and which illustrate some of the points made.

Case One. A bitch aged two years, in her first pregnancy. Labour started normally on the sixty-second day after service. It proceeded uneventfully until eight puppies had been born. The bitch then settled down happily with her litter of healthy normal puppies, and fed them satisfactorily. She looked rather large, but no more puppies could be felt by abdominal examination. On the second day the bitch was taking her food and the puppies were thriving. Only six had been kept. On the morning of the third day after whelping, a seventh puppy was found, dead, in the box. During this day the bitch was watched very carefully, and was seen to strain when passing water, but not otherwise. A vaginal examination revealed, at the extreme limit of reach, a rounded hairy surface which could be identified as not being a head. The membranes had clearly been ruptured and the puppy was in an abnormal position. The passages were still fully dilated. A single dose of pituitrin was injected, which produced strong pains but no advance of the puppy. Operative treatment was decided on, and since the puppy could be reached from the vagina it was decided to extract it by this route.

As the puppy was certain to be dead, and the bitch not in difficulties, it was thought best to give her some hours' rest after the examinations she had had. She was then anaesthetized and with the consequent relaxation of all her tissues, it could be felt that the puppy was lying with one shoulder as the presenting part, too high for successful turning. It was removed piecemeal, without injury of any kind to the bitch. It was before the days of penicillin, or she would have received treatment with this, but she made an uninterrupted recovery, and the six puppies throve and had no setback of any kind.

This case illustrates two important points. First, that of careful observation; unless the straining had been noticed, the presence of yet another dead puppy might not have been suspected until decomposition had set in, with serious consequences for the bitch. Second, had the puppy not been palpable from the vagina, it could not have been extracted by this route.

Case Two.   A bitch agd six years, and third pregnancy. Her two previous litters had consisted of twelve puppies in each case, and births had been normal. On the sixty-third day she showed no signs of imminent whelping, her previous litters had been born on the sixty-second day. By the sixty-fourth day there were still no signs of whelping, and the veterinary surgeon was called in. He advised leaving her for another twenty-four hours. On the sixty-fifth day the bitch became restless and uncomfortable, but this passed off, then recurred and passed off again. Although the passages were fairly well dilated, no puppy could be felt in the vagina. A single dose of pituitrin was given, and though this brought on good contractions there was no advance. A high obstruction was diagnosed, and an immediate Caesarian decided on.

Only four puppies were present, all alive, though unfortunately none survived. It should be mentioned that this was before the day of the more modern anaesthetics. Present-day drugs give a much better chance of survival.

The obstruction in this case was caused by the first puppy lying across the axis of the uterus, with head extended, so that the entire back was presenting, and the puppy could not possibly pass through the pelvic brim. In such a position natural delivery was impossible, and a Caesarian operation the only means of extracting the puppy.

This case forms a useful contrast to the first, and illustrates once more the importance of early diagnosis, and also the fact that unless a puppy can be felt through the vagina, it is impossible to deliver it through the external passages. It also shows the value of this operation at a time when it is likely to be successful. Too often it is regarded as a last desperate resort, to be undertaken only when other methods of effecting delivery have been tried in vain. At this stage the bitch will be exhausted and almost certainly infected, and the hope of a happy outcome will be small. A Caesarian operation is life-saving when undertaken at an early stage, when the bitch is in good condition, has not run any great risk of infection by repeated manual examinations and the puppies have not suffered as the result of pressure.

Both these cases serve to highlight the advances in both prevention of sepsis and also Caesarian section. Today both cases would have been operated on as soon as the difficulties had been diagnosed.

Treatment of Abnormal Labour

Treatment of abnormal whelping is the province of the veterinary surgeon. He alone has the training and experience to deal with it, and the knowledge to assess the possibilities.

He alone is in the position to advise on treatment and to carry it out. But even an elementary appreciation of the factors and risks involved will help the breeder to decide between the courses which may be presented to him. His is the ultimate decision on what, if anything, is to be done. The more he understands all that is involved, the more likely he is to come to a wise decision, and the more confidence he will feel that he and his veterinary surgeon are working in a way as a team in the attempt to save a serious situation.

Some of the factors which will guide the choice of treatment are as follows:

Pelvic Abnormalities in the Bitch.   Any history of bone disease in puppyhood or any accidents which may have resulted in narrowing of the pelvis should indicate a careful examination by your veterinary surgeon. If you desperately want a puppy from this particular bitch, provided pregnancy can be achieved, a Caesarian section offers the most likely chance of a living litter.

The Degree of Dilatation of Vagina and Cervix.   From what has been said previously it is clear that this is an important factor in considering any treatment. Unless the cervix and vagina are fully dilated it is impossible to use instruments safely and it may be disastrous to give any violent stimulus to uterine contraction. Pituitrin is the remedy for a sluggish uterus when the preliminary stage of dilatation has proceeded normally; it is a valuable drug when used with care and the knowledge of local conditions which it demands. It is not a drug to be used in a hit-or-miss attempt at delivery.

Uterine Inertia.   We have seen that inertia may occur from intrinsic causes, due to the absence of hormone stimulation, and alternatively to exhaustion following on prolonged activity. In the first case, and provided that the passages are dilated, pituitrin is valuable. It is not unknown for an injection to be needed to expel every puppy in a severe case of primary inertia. In the case of an exhausted uterus, pituitrin is useless, the uterus has lost its contractile power. Even if this power is temporarily regained after a period of rest, the original obstruction still remains, and pituitrin is actively dangerous and may lead to a ruptured uterus.

In any state of exhaustion owing to an obstruction, the most sensible course to take is to allow the bitch to rest quietly for some hours to enable the uterus to recover its tone, and then to have a Caesarian operation performed. Breeders should never allow this serious condition to develop, and should call in expert help at once when signs of difficult whelping arise.

Presence of the Presenting Part in the Vagina. This will decide whether forceps can be used, or whether a Caesarian operation is the wiser choice, and in these days of better anaesthetics and better techniques, the latter is usually performed in most cases of such difficulties.

The general condition of the bitch has an important bearing on questions of treatment of obstructed labour. Should she have been in labour for a prolonged period, and should she have undergone repeated examinations and attempts at delivery, sepsis is almost a certainty, and this, with her exhaustion, makes the outlook grave, whatever treatment is adopted. Things should never be allowed to come to this dreadful pass.

The preceding section has involved some recapitulation. The subjects dealt with, however, are of such vital importance to safe whelping that they cannot be over-emphasized, and repetition may serve to drive them home.

One further question remains to be considered.

Safe Emergency Methods for Breeders

Advice has been constantly given that the veterinary surgeon should be consulted in all cases of difficulty, and this advice always holds good. But occasions may occur when need is urgent but veterinary help not available, or at any rate not available within a reasonable period of time. How much then, in the way of help, can the lay breeder safely give to bitches in difficulties?

No hard and fast rules can be laid down; much must depend on circumstances, and more on the breeder's experience. It is safe to say that, in the absence of skilled help, it is better to do too little than too much. But there are conditions in which a little help may save the life of a puppy.

As a rough-and-ready guide one might say that when a puppy is within easy reach of the examining finger, or when part of its anatomy is already born, as in the case of a breech birth, the attendant should do what he can to help delivery.

The use of any kinds of instruments should be strictly confined to the veterinary surgeon.

Unborn puppies are extremely slippery; it is almost impossible to get a firm grip with the bare hand. A small square of boiled lint, or a boiled white cotton glove, will help in securing and maintaining a firm hold.

It is important to pull gently, and continuously. The bitch will then help by contracting and pushing until the puppy is born. Do not use excessive force. If the puppy cannot be birthed in this way, veterinary advice is essential.

The most usual event needing help is a breech birth with delay of the after-coming head. In the normal head-down position, the head, the largest part of the puppy at birth, stretches the passages to their fullest extent, and the body and quarters, being smaller, slip out easily with the next contraction. But when the tail end is born first, the rump may emerge before full dilatation has been reached, and the larger head may have difficulty in following.

If the body is held firmly with the covered hand, taking great care not to squeeze or crush the fragile bones and delicate tissues, and traction is applied gently with a pain, the head can usually be extracted without too much trouble.

The danger of delay is that the placenta will almost certainly have separated, and the puppy will therefore be cut off from its oxygen supply before it can take in air by breathing. If the head is not extracted and the mouth freed so that the puppy can breathe, it will die from asphyxia.

A large head in proportion to the body may give the same trouble, and can be dealt with in the same way.

Reviving Puppies.　Many puppies are born in poor shape. This may be due to pressure after prolonged labour, or to premature separation of the placenta, cutting off oxygen supplies before the lungs are functioning. Puppies born by Caesarian operation sometimes died from the effects of the anaesthetic given to the dam, because they could not be got to breathe. Improved methods now make this much less likely. Puppies which are blue and limp at birth will die unless steps are taken to restore them. Puppies born white and flaccid are usually beyond help. The first thing to be done is to see that the mouth is free from membrane, and, if not, free it with the finger. Opening the mouth gently may itself stimulate the puppy to gasp. Any fluid in the mouth should be wiped gently away if possible, and the puppy taken on to the lap on a warm rough towel, and then rubbed briskly though gently for a few moments, rubbing the wrong way of the hair has seemed to the writer especially stimulating. Alternating with rubbing, gentle swinging of the puppy can be tried, grasping it firmly round the body and gently swinging it through an arc, which acts as a form of artificial respiration. A trace of ammonia held near the nostrils will often cause the puppy to gasp, and once air has entered the lungs, normal respiration usually starts. Some sort of stimulation which causes the puppy to take a breath or gasp for air is needed, and dipping alternatively in hot and cold water is sometimes recommended. The writer has found the remedies mentioned successful in cases where any success was possible.

Once the lungs are expanded by a few breaths, the ominous dusky colour of the skin surfaces and mucus membranes will gradually give place to the normal pink, as oxygen finds its way into the blood stream. The bitch's licking will usually complete the stimulation needed.

Such puppies are not necessarily weaklings, and once revived and made to breathe, they are quite normal.

5

Puppy Rearing

Apart from food, the most important single factor in the life of a young puppy is warmth. Even allowing for the normal fall of 1–2°C. or 2–3°F. shortly before whelping, the change of temperature from that within the bitch's body to that of an unheated room or kennel is immense, and the normal heat-regulating mechanism of the puppy's own body does not come into action for some time.

Any structure which is dry and weather proof, and which can be kept warm day and night can be used for the bitch and her litter.[1] Fresh air and sunshine enter into the picture after a couple of weeks, and convenience in siting is important to the owner.

The kitchen, or any warm room in the house, is ideal for whelping, and puppies can live there until they become very active and are constantly in and out of their nest, when it is obviously not so convenient, but by that time some outside building can probably be adapted for them.

Breeders on a large scale must obviously have one or more permanent puppyhouses. Those able to build these for the special purpose will have their own ideas. The essentials are soundness of structure, with freedom from draughts, some source of permanent heating, and the writer believes electricity to be the safest, and a convector heater the most effective. The infr-red lamp is now much used, especially for piglets and puppies, and appears to be most successful. It is suspended above the nest, at the distance recommended in instructions, and must not be used at a lower level than that indicated. Sunshine and good ventilation are needed for the ideal puppyhouse, with adequate space for a bed large enough to hold them until they are ready to go to their new owners at the age of eight or nine weeks. There must be room also for a

[1] A minimum temperature of 24°C. (75°F.) is recommended.

separate bed for the bitch, out of the reach of puppies. She will need this as the puppies get bigger, and worry her too much; there must be floor space for the litter to play when the weather is bad, and lastly an outside run, fenced in, preferably with linked netting, with a door between it and the puppy-house, and shade from hot sun, in the shape of a tree or a screen contrived by the breeder.

Flooring may be of wood, concrete or breeze blocks, or some of the newer materials. Ease of cleaning is a consideration. The writer has always used concrete for both house and run and has found it quite satisfactory. It is disliked by some breeders, but puppies do not lie about on concrete if a good warm bed is provided, except in very hot weather when it does them no harm, and it wears down toe nails and keeps feet tight and pasterns firm, in a way soft ground can never do.

Bedding

Although woodwool makes a good bedding for puppies, thought should be given to one of the acrylic fibre fur fabrics (for example VetBed) since these are hygienic, not allergic and do not get into the puppies' coats. Sawdust, which often looks nice on kennel floors, can be quite dangerous. It gets into their food, their eyes, noses and coats. Even when it is used solely in the sanitary area, its disadvantages probably outweigh its usefulness. Puppies can quite easily and quickly be trained to newspaper, which is possibly cheaper and just as effective as a hygienic means of removing excrement.

Feeding

Protein. The puppy, as well as the nursing bitch, should have a high protein diet. This is a fundamental of good rearing. Protein is that part of the food essential for building the animal body during growth and for repair and renewal of tissues throughout life. The main sources are meat, fish, eggs etc. and milk casein. These are first class proteins. Second class proteins are less digestible, e.g. tendon, lights etc. as well as the protein of root vegetables, peas and beans etc. Vegetable protein is often accompanied by large amounts of carbohydrate in the form of starch and although this is a useful energy source for the dog it is not a natural source which is provided by fats as found in meat. Good supplies of high quality protein together with adequate energy sources are essential during pregnancy and lactation but energy foods, starches and fats, should not be fed to excess, otherwise the bitch will become obese.

Fat. The third main constituent of food, fat provides the body with heat by its combustion in the tissues, and animal fat is valuable because it contains the Vitamins A and D. When meat or milk are absent from the diet, cod-liver oil is probably the best substitute, owing to its Vitamin A and D content.

Mineral. Many minerals are essential to the animal body. Iron, calcium (lime), phosphorus, iodine and so on, and traces of others, such as cobalt, are equally essential. These are known as trace minerals. Green vegetables, preferably raw, are a useful source of these minerals, and these can be finely shredded and mixed with the food. Spinach seems especially liked by dogs, and parsley contains much Vitamin A.

The calcium-phosphorus ratio is of the greatest importance in developing good bone. Very little true bone is present at birth, the bones themselves being soft and largely composed of either membrane or cartilage. Calcification, or ossification, as it is called, occurs after birth, and is not complete until maturity. During this period true bone continues to be laid down, and the process is controlled by Vitamin D acting on the calcium-phosphorus ratio.

The Vitamins. Vitamins are usually protein substances or complicated fatty acids, found in natural foodstuffs, which are essential to the growth, health and proper function of the animal body. They are now so well known that they need only to be briefly summarized here. Some vitamins are manufactured in the body itself, others are supplied by diet. If this were perfectly satisfactory in all respects, no additional supplies would be needed. But with the many forms of processed food of today, human as well as canine, we cannot always be sure that the essential vitamins have survived in the finished product, and supplements may be needed, especially in illness, pregnancy and puppy rearing.

The main vitamins concerned in puppy breeding are:

Vitamin A, needed for growth and resistance to infection. It is fat soluble, and is found in egg yolk, halibut- and cod-liver oils, milk, butter, liver, kidney, carrots (as carotene) and many green vegetables. It is dangerous when given in great excess.

Vitamin D, also fat soluble and, like A, dangerous in excess, is concerned in bone development, in conjunction with calcium and phosphorus, which cannot be utilized by the body in its absence. It is unique among vitamins, in that it can be absorbed through the skin, by the action of sunlight on exposed areas. Such areas are, of course, few in the dog. Vitamin D is associated with Vitamin A in egg yolk, fish oils, especially sardines, which are rich in this vitamin, milk, butter and magarine (in which a high percentage is incorporated by law). By using foods fortified with Vitamin D, and giving in addition supplementary doses in various preparations, it is easy to give a harmful amount and this should be born in mind in puppy rearing.

Vitamin C, the anti-scurvy vitamin, is found in fruits, green vegetables, germinating peas and beans, and in potatoes in the layer immediately beneath the skin. Fruit and green vegetables were known to be a cure for this now rare disease long before the existence of Vitamin C was even suspected. Dogs normally manufacture Vitamin C in their own tissues, and a deficiency is very rare.

Vitamin B consists of a complex series of many separate substances, all of great importance to health. A number of serious diseases are caused by a lack of one or other of the B group. B Vitamins are very widely distributed in foodstuffs, occurring in meat, especially liver, fish, egg yolk, peas and beans, all wholegrain cereals, and yeast. Unlike the other members of the series, B. 2 (Riboflavin) is found in green vegetables. It would appear that brewers' yeast provides the best single source of the complex, and Vetzyme, known to all dog breeders, is a valuable preparation of the Vitamin B group.

Vitamin E was originally described as the fertility vitamin. Later research, however, casts some doubt on its action. Little is known of its requirements or of the results of deficiency, but although its role in the animal economy is uncertain, research may eventually provide more information.

Vitamin K is concerned with the mechanism of blood clotting, which it affects indirectly, and through the action of body chemistry. In the dog it is manufactured by the normal bacteria in the gut and provided bile is being normally produced is absorbed readily. It can prove useful if there are clotting deficiencies, especially if the dog has eaten Warfarin rat poison when Vitamin K acts as a specific antidote.

Feeding the Nursing Bitch

If the breeder remembers that during the nine weeks of pre-natal life, and for the first two or three weeks after birth, the bitch must not only maintain and restore her own tissues, but supply all the material needed to form the bodies of any number from two or three to ten or twelve puppies (though it is to be hoped that one bitch may never be asked to feed such a number), he will realize that she must be properly fed, and this means a high protein diet, that is, a diet rich in meat, milk, fish and eggs. She will then be in good condition to feed her puppies without depleting her own resources unduly. The well-being and development of the litter will depend on the amount and quality of the dam's milk, providing numbers are kept within reasonable bounds.

For the first few days after whelping the bitch's food should be milk and milky preparations, barley, groats, Farex, or something of the kind, with perhaps egg yolk added. Tripe and fish can be given if the bitch will take them. Raw meat, if possible, should be restored after two or three days; it is not only the easiest way of giving protein, but it also stimulates milk production. Milk, fortified in the manner to be described shortly, can be given in amounts as large as the bitch will take, and four good meals daily, two of milk with cereal and egg, and two of meat will not be too much. Fish can be substituted for meat two or three times a week, but should not entirely take its place. Cod- or halibut-liver oil may be added, in one or two teasoonful doses for cod-liver oil, and two to three drops halibut, in one feed daily. Extra lime and phosphorus can be given in the form of 'Stress', a mineral product made by Phillips Yeast Products. Clean drinking water should be available at all times. The amount of food needed is decided by the size of the bitch and the number of puppies in the litter. She should never be stinted.

It is often difficult to coax maternally minded bitches from their nests for the first day or two, and the writer has always fed bitches in their beds during this short time if they prefer it. But they must be taken out to relieve themselves, on a lead if necessary. Once outside there is no trouble, and the bitch will rejoin her puppies the moment she is ready.

Ample feeding should continue for the first four to five weeks, after which the amount can be gradually reduced as the puppies begin to feed themselves. By the time they are completely weaned, the dam's diet should be back to normal. The writer's experience is that apart from visiting the puppies to relieve the supply of milk once or twice daily, bitches do not suckle their puppies after about six weeks, but they regurgitate their food for some little time longer.

Bitches which will not eat present a serious problem. A veterinary surgeon should be consulted, and the owner must try to find something the dam will eat and enjoy, whatever it may be. Sardines are often accepted, or other delicacies may be found. Just as the appetite grows in eating, so the disinclination for food grows with fasting, and this vicious circle should not be allowed to establish itself if it can be avoided.

Puppy Rearing

Puppy rearing does not start with the birth of a litter. It does not start even with the mating of the bitch. It may be considered as a continuous process. In order to rear strong puppies the bitch must herself be well grown and well fed. This entails proper care from birth onwards. Puppy rearing may be looked on as an endless chain, the puppy of this year being the parent of the future and so on indefinitely.

Throughout the puppy stage, until the maximum growth has been attained, the great essential is to keep the animal growing on without a check. Any serious interruption may be difficult to make up. Even in breeds in which size should be as small as possible it is highly unwise to underfeed puppies in order to keep it down. This happens in some small breeds, and usually results in weedy animals.

Provided the bitch has good supplies of milk and is settling down happily with her litter, the puppies will need nothing else for the first fortnight of their lives, and the only event in the period (apart from removing dew claws and docking when required) is the opening of eyes. This normally takes place between the ninth and the fourteenth day. While the eyes are opening, and this occurs gradually over two or three days, they should not be exposed to bright light, and even for the next week it is wiser to avoid strong sunlight.

During the third week the puppies should be taught to lap, though at this early age this procedure is a lesson rather than an addition to their diet. The following table shows the difference in composition between the milk of bitch, cow and goat.

	Fat	Protein	Carbohydrate (Lactose)
Bitch	8.3	7.5	3.7
Cow	3.9	3.5	4.9
Goat	4.1	3.6	5.1

As can be seen from the table the chief differences between the milk of the bitch and the cow is that the bitch's milk contains twice as much protein and more than twice as much fat. Goat's milk is marginally better in this respect than cow's milk. If human baby foods are being used to feed the puppy in the absence of Lactol or Whelpi these should be *made up at double strength.* Nevertheless they are not ideal since the amount of milk-sugar, lactose, present is much greater than in bitch's milk and can cause diarrhoea. It is much easier to start weaning using one of the simulated bitch's milks which can be gradually diluted and then cow's milk substituted after a week or so.

Feed each pup with a teaspoonful of this prepared milk. This is most easily done on the lap out of a shallow saucer. Many puppies lap at once without hesitation. Others indulge in a good deal of sucking and blowing before they get the knack of lapping, but they all become proficient in a very short time.

As the days go on the amount given can be increased; this will reduce the strain on the bitch and prepare the way for weaning, as well as being a definite contribution to the pups' nutrition.

At the same time as they are being taught to lap, meat can be introduced. First try raw scraped meat since most puppies will take this avidly, then one of the proprietary puppy foods can be offered, Pedigree Puppy Chum or similar. As soon as puppies are used to solid food each puppy must get its fair share and the best way of ensuring this is to feed in separate dishes if the litter is small or to feed in twos and threes.

Egg yolk can be given at the time meat is introduced or even earlier. The reason for using yolk alone is this; raw egg white contains an antivitaminic substance called avidin, which destroys one of the B vitamins called biotin, and while it would probably take a large amount of the first to kill all the biotin in the system, feeding raw yolk alone ensures that no biotin is unnecessarily lost. Egg whites may be boiled, chopped up and safely fed in this form, for cooking destroys avidin. One egg yolk between four puppies can be used as a start, increasing the amount gradually.

By this age puppies are very active, and should be out in the sun when possible, with some shade provided.

The automatic action of bladder and bowel is established and puppies will relieve themselves after every meal. The opportunity of starting house training should be taken, by putting them out, or on to a heap of sawdust, and so establishing the habit of cleanliness.

Drinking water should also be supplied, for puppies will drink a lot, and if they grow up drinking nothing but milk, it is sometimes difficult to persuade them to take water.

At five weeks old two milk meals and one of meat or fish can be given, still gradually increasing the amount. Fish should always be cooked. Herrings are excellent, and can be minced up, later broken up, bones and all. Bones must be removed from all other kinds of fish. By this time the bitch will be away from her puppies for comparatively long periods, and, though she will like to play with them, she will probably not want to feed them except perhaps morning, evening and mid-day. She will also vomit her partially digested food for them to eat, a warning that a milk diet is no longer adequate for the puppies.

This process is entirely natural, and all bitches seem to use it for weaning their offspring. The writer has had one or two greedy bitches, however, who, after vomiting a meal, gobbled it up again themselves and would not let the puppies go near it. These were all excellent mothers and devoted to their children.

So far starch and starchy foods have not been mentioned in puppy diet, and the writer believes that it is best avoided until at least the age of six weeks, in favour of the concentrated and highly nutritious foodstuffs already mentioned. The old days of feeding puppies on bread and watered milk are over as far as knowledgeable breeders are concerned, or so we must hope, but some breeders still fill tiny puppy stomachs with starchy food, bread, porridge and so on, even potatoes. This leads to indigestion and malnutrition, a serious matter in young puppies.

At the age of six weeks feeds may be arranged as follows, the bitch leaving the litter early in the morning.

8–9 a.m.	Prepared milk, beaten egg yolk added, one to every three puppies.
11 a.m.	Noon. Minced meat or broken-up fish, mixed with a little fine biscuit meal well soaked, or brown bread crumbs, one drop of halibut-oil for each pup. Meal must be thoroughly soaked but not sloppy.
2 p.m.	Bitch should visit her puppies, if she has no milk she will probably vomit her food for them.
5 p.m.	A milk feed as at 8.0 a.m., but without egg. A hard biscuit or a big bone after this, but nothing which could splinter.

8 p.m.   A good feed of minced meat with one Vetzyme
tablet.

10–11 p.m.   Bitch to be returned for the night.

She should now have a bed which the puppies cannot
reach.

No specified amount of any foods can be given in general
directions of this kind; these will vary with the breed and the
age and size of the puppies. It is a safe rule to give just as much
as the puppies will eat greedily, and never to leave any food
lying about.

The Post-Weaning Period

At the age of about seven weeks it is unlikely that the bitch will
have milk left, and in any case it is wise to have the puppies
completely weaned before they are eight weeks old. Meals
should still be given every three hours, and this continued
until the pups are ten weeks old. Some will have gone to new
homes by this time, and a careful diet sheet should have been
given, with full directions for continuing and increasing the
amounts as required, as well as adding other items. Amounts
of food should be steadily increased, a growing puppy needs
more food for its weight than an adult, and though growth has
slowed down by now, it is still taking place, bones are hardening from the deposition of calcium in their substance and
muscles are developing.

By ten to twelve weeks ordinary fresh cows' milk may be
substituted for the reinforced milk the puppies have been
having. Plenty of meat is still the rule, it may be varied with
tripe, fish, liver or any animal food, and finely shredded green
vegetables may be added. Cod- or halibut-oil should be continued, and eggs are most valuable. Vetzyme must be
continued.

At ten to twelve weeks feeds may be reduced to four daily,
with an extra drink of milk. The mineral product Stress is still
necessary, for at this time the bones are becoming calcified,
and the second teeth are forming in the gums.

Between four and five months feeds can be cut to three
daily, with of course increased amounts and extra milk. Meals

should be of high quality, for at this age puppies may tend to get leggy and thin, and may lose condition unless really well fed. It is about the worst age at which to judge what the mature puppy will look like.

Many puppies lose their appetites at this time, and the first thing to think of is a sore mouth, with swollen gums and a permanent tooth about to come through. Some puppies cut their permanent teeth with no trouble at all, others have a difficult and painful time, and a veterinary surgeon should be consulted in such cases.

Competition between two or more dogs in the matter of food is often helpful, particularly with slow or shy feeders. Wherever possible diet should not be changed too often since the bowel flora or germs in the bowel live in status quo with their environment and if there are violent changes in the food swallowed, violent changes in gut bugs can result in equally violent diarrhoea!

Exercise

So far we have not considered the question of exercise. Organized exercise does not enter into the life of young puppies, which will get all they need by playing together, and there should always be some space provided where they can romp as much as they like. Puppies do not overdo this, they alternate between riotous play and complete rest. Natural play provides the exercise needed to develop muscles, strengthen joints and to stimulate the circulation, which supplies nourishment to all the tissues of the body. Owners of a single puppy should remember this, and find some form of activity, such as throwing a ball, hiding and letting the puppy find them, or anything else they can devise. The ideal is to have two puppies which will play with each other, or perhaps an older, but not too old, dog which will join in the games.

Balls should be of solid rubber, and should always be of such a size that they could not possibly be swallowed.

Rest is as necessary for a puppy as exercise, and is often forgotten, especially in a household with children, who will often wear a young puppy out by never allowing it to rest.

The care of puppies can be wonderful training for children, but it must be under supervision until the children are old enough to realize their responsibilities in the matter. Rest and play alternately form, with eating, the natural rhythm of the puppy's life.

6

Puppy Management

Size of Litters

How many puppies should a bitch be required to rear? This problem naturally affects only breeds which normally have large litters, ten, twelve, or more. It is no answer to maintain that Nature provides sustenance for all puppies born. Nature allows for a high wastage which does not occur with good breeding and rearing methods. The strain of feeding a big litter tries the bitch considerably and leads to loss of condition. Moreover the cost of feeding puppies from five or six weeks onwards is heavy in such breeds, and becomes enormous if puppies of the larger breeds which are normally those with big litters have not been sold by the age of eight or nine weeks.

The writer believes that six or seven puppies is the optimum number, unless the breed is so rare that it is essential to increase numbers, as in the case of mastiffs after the war. The choice will then lie between a foster-mother and hand rearing.

Foster-Mothers

A foster-mother should be carefully chosen. The ideal is a newly whelped bitch, known to the breeder to be suitable in size, health, temperament and freedom from parasites. The question of temperament is often overlooked, but is important. Although tendencies are in-born, puppies are imitative, and learn much of their behaviour from the example of their dam or foster-mother. The breeder who can find the ideal bitch is fortunate, but bitches in phantom pregnancy often will make ideal foster mothers.

Care is needed in introducing her new family to the foster-bitch. If her own puppies are with her (and they should not be more than a day or two older than those she is to adopt) she should be taken away and the new pups well mixed with her own to acquire their scent. A drop or two of malt extract or milk on their coats may encourage the bitch to lick them, and once she has done this she will usually take them on without further trouble. She should not, however, be left until it is clear that she has accepted them. Her own puppies should be removed gradually, one at a time, and humanely disposed of. If the foster-mother is needed only in order to rear a large litter, the best puppies should be left with their own mother.

Hand Rearing

This method of rearing is usually only resorted to in cases of necessity, such as the death of the bitch, her illness, or complete failure of the milk supply. It involves the breeder in devotion to a full-time task for the first week or two, but is often very successful, and hand-reared puppies are among many of our big winners.

Warmth is essential; this can be provided with hot-water bottles in an emergency or by an infra-red lamp— but remember that the natural environment is very damp due to the bitch continuously licking and cleaning her puppies. Therefore it is advantageous to provide a damp towel, or something similar, in one corner of the whelping box to give the necessary humidity particularly when an infra-red lamp is used.

Feeds should be two-hourly through the day for the first week, but provided a warm, humid nest is provided, puppies will go through the night from, say, midnight until 6 a.m. without feeding. After the first week the interval between feeding can be gradually increased. Simulated bitch's milk (Lactol, Whelpi etc.) is probably best but alternatively human baby formula made up to double strength will suffice. It is worthwhile laying in a stock of bitch's milk replacement in case of emergencies. A Catac open-ended feeder or a Belcroy feeder obtainable from your veterinary surgeon are convenient for feeding orphan puppies but in emergency a dropper or small hypodermic syringe (5 ml) without its needle attached can be used. The formula must be warmed to about

38°C. (100°F.) and the bottle must be wrapped up to retain the heat and gently shaken from time to time to distribute the cream.

Evacuations are a problem. For the first few days of life puppies pass water only when stimulated by the bitch's licking. This must be imitated as far as possible by a piece of lint wrapped round a finger and used in the same way after every feed, and at constant intervals. The entry of food into the stomach sets up a chain of reflexes which result in evacuation of the bowel, and all young puppies defecate after every meal. (This can later be used as a basis for house training.) The breeder must take the place of the bitch in keeping the bed clean, by removing all excreta.

Constipation or diarrhoea can occur with hand-feeding. A few drops of liquid paraffin may be helpful as can baby's Gripe Water. Remember liquid paraffin can coat the bowel and prevent absorption of oil soluble vitamins therefore it should never be given for more than a day or two. Diarrhoea is more serious. Scrupulous attention to cleanliness, boiling of bottles and teats and freshly prepared food may prevent it, and a change of diet may be indicated. A veterinary surgeon should always be consulted in any serious case of diarrhoea.

The Disposal of Unwanted Puppies

This is always distressing to the dog lover, who cannot help feeling responsible for the lives he has caused to be born. It may be essential in the interests of the majority. There is no kindness in keeping weaklings, or puppies with malformations, and mismarked puppies are best destroyed in the interests of the breed. Most responsible breeders keep only those puppies which they know they can rear well.

Unwanted puppies should be taken to the veterinary surgeon as soon as possible after birth in order that they can be humanely euthanased. None of the 'do-it-yourself' methods of puppy euthanasia are satisfactory, neither on humane nor aesthetic grounds. Drowning should certainly not be resorted to.

Removal of Dewclaws

This operation is best performed as soon after birth as possible and certainly not beyond the fourth day of life. Ideally it should be done by a veterinary surgeon, although breeders can undertake the task themselves. I would however suggest a novice always seeks the help of someone who has experience.

Dewclaws are the rudimentary thumbs, set above the other digits, and occur on the forelegs and occasionally on the hindlegs. If not taken off, they can be troublesome, for the nails have nothing to wear them down. Apart from sometimes growing into the leg, dewclaws also can cause trouble by inflicting nasty wounds, especially on children, if the dog is at all boisterous. However, do remember that breed standards in some cases (for example Pyreneans), state that dewclaws (in this case hind) should be left.

A pair of straight, blunt-pointed surgical scissors or nailcutters should be used. Friar's balsam, permanganate of potash or tincture of perchloride of iron can be used to stop bleeding. Boil the instruments before use and leave them in the boiled water until needed. Although the job can be done single-handed, it is easier if someone holds the puppy, with the leg extended towards you. Scissors or clippers should be placed parallel with the leg, with the whole tiny joint between the blades. A piece of cotton wool moistened with the styptic, or with a few granules of permanganate of potash, must be placed firmly on the wound in order to stop bleeding. Providing the operation is carried out fairly soon after birth, puppies do not seem to feel any pain. However, the older the puppy, the more barbarous the operation appears. Certainly later in life it is a major operation that should be done by a veterinary surgeon under a general anaesthetic.

Docking

Docking is now considered by many members of the veterinary profession to be a mutilative operation that should not be performed. However, while breed standards still call for the docking of puppies' tails, it is wise to endeavour to secure expert help before the operation is attempted.

Again, it should be carried out before the fourth day of life. With healthy puppies, I endeavour to do it as soon after birth as possible, believing that if the shock of the operation can be telescoped into the shock of birth, this is all the better for the puppy. If it is not possible to secure veterinary help, make sure of the assistance of an experienced breeder.

Nail Trimming

Puppy nails grow fast, and from the first week onwards should be trimmed regularly every few days with a pair of nail scissors. There is nothing to wear them down in the nest, and they quickly become so long and sharp that the puppies scratch each other and their mother. It is not unusual to find sores on the backs of some puppies during the second week, made by the clawing of other members of the litter in dragging themselves over the backs of the first comers to get to the bitch. These sores disappear if nails are kept trimmed, and as soon as the puppies are on their legs.

This possibility should be remembered if a normal good-tempered bitch should suddenly appear to take a dislike to her puppies and resent feeding them. She may be found to be badly scratched and even infected by the puppies needle-sharp nails.

Care must be taken not to cut into the quick in trimming nails. This is easily seen when they are light, not so apparent in dark nails. The easiest way of trimming is to hold the puppy on the lap, controlling it with the left forearm and holding the foot out with the thumb and fingers of the same hand.

Running about on a hard surface soon wears the nails down naturally when feet are round and compact and toes well arched. The nails of long, thin-toed feet do not wear down so easily.

Cropped Ears

The Kennel Club will not register any dog with cropped ears that has been born within its jurisdiction or born outside such jurisdiction but had its ears cropped within its jurisdiction.

Any puppies born from such dogs would also be ineligible

for registration. Imported dogs with cropped ears can of course be registered and thus shown under KC regulations.

Teething

Dogs have two sets of teeth. The first, milk, or deciduous, teeth have no roots and are shed at the age of four or five months in most breeds. They begin to erupt at about three weeks, and are usually all cut by the end of the fifth week of life.

Milk teeth are twenty-eight in number and are softer and sharper than the permanent teeth. They are also more widely spaced, and it is difficult to tell from their position whether the bite will be correct. In all breeds except those which should be undershot, the permanent teeth should meet, the upper incisors touching and slightly overlapping the lower, forming the scissor bite. An edge to edge bite, in which upper and lower incisors meet edge to edge, is not desired, it denotes a lower jaw which is slightly too long. In the undershot bite the lower incisors project beyond the upper, and may not even touch them. The converse of this, the overshot, or pig jaw as it is sometimes called, is also incorrect.

Even during the first dentition either condition may be suspected by looking at the puppy in profile, when the protrusion of either upper or lower jaw can be observed. If the set of the jaws is level it is not likely that the puppy will be either over- or under-shot at maturity.

The permanent teeth begin to erupt at from three to four months of age in most medium and large breeds. Toy breeds are usually later. The upper molars are the first to appear, the upper incisors showing at about the same time or a day or two later, followed by the lower molars and the lower incisors. There are forty-two or forty-four teeth in all in the permanent dentition, the last to erupt are usually the canines, and these are very deeply rooted and may give trouble.

The milk teeth usually loosen and fall out, but are sometimes slow in doing so, and may cause the permanent teeth to be badly aligned, unless they are removed. Any temporary teeth still firmly fixed in the jaw after the permanent teeth have come through should be removed, a veterinary surgeon should be consulted about this.

The eruption of permanent teeth may be difficult and cause much pain. When a healthy puppy refuses food at this time the teeth and mouth should always be examined, for this is the most likely cause of lack of appetite.

Some Hereditary Defects

Entropion. A condition in which one or both eyelids, upper and lower, are inverted or turned in, in such a way that the eyelashes constantly brush the surface of the eye [the cornea], causing intense discomfort and irritation. If the condition is allowed to persist it will lead to ulceration of the cornea and ultimately to blindness.

Entropion may be due to developmental causes, from a narrowed space between upper and lower lids, and this is the usual reason for the defect. But it can be due to accident or injury causing a scar with subsequent contraction of the tissue. It is most frequently found in breeds in which small deeply set eyes are required, but may occur in any other.

Surgical treatment is the only satisfactory method of dealing with entropion.

Cleft Palate. This may be due to accidents of development in the embryo resulting in failure of the tissues of the palate to close in the midline. A genetic basis can sometimes be suspected, particularly if a number of cases recur in the same strain or breed. In Bulldogs it may occur as a simple recessive. Both hard and soft palate may be involved, resulting in a communication between the mouth and the nasal cavity. It is often associated with hare lip, an extension of the defect to the external structure of the face. Cleft palate is most common in short-faced breeds, and is noticeable from birth, as puppies affected are unable to suck properly; milk is returned through the nose accompanied by froth. Such puppies are unlikely to survive and should not be allowed to do so. Operative treatment is difficult and unlikely to be successful.

Deafness. It is only recently that veterinary scientists have started to unravel the complexities of deafness in dogs although deafness in the Dalmatian has been known for many

years as a recurrent problem. However, its mode of inheritance
is still improperly understood and is certainly not simple.
Obviously, puppies should not be bred from deaf parents.
parents.

Deafness should be suspected if, by the age of four weeks,
any puppy should take no notice of sudden noises; normal
puppies are alert if a door opens or a food bowl rattles, and
still more if a whistle is blown unexpectedly. Every little head
will then go up—except that of a deaf puppy.

A few days' observation will in all probability confirm the
sad fact. A veterinary surgeon should be consulted but even
then positive confirmation of partial deafness is very often difficult to establish. If there is any doubt it is better not to sell the
puppy and tragic though it may be, to have it humanely
destroyed.

Progressive Retinal Atrophy or hereditary blindness is known
today to exist in two forms: generalised or peripheral, which in
every breed afflicted has been proven to be due to a recessive
gene; and Central PRA which differs from the generalised
form in that affected animals often seem to be able to see better
in dim light than bright light. Generalised PRA can also be
termed night blindness. CPRA is not so widespread as PRA
and appears to affect mainly working dogs, Collies and
Retrievers having the highest incidence, whereas PRA affects
Cockers, Miniature and Toy Poodles, Dachshunds, Elkhounds,
to mention but a few. The exact mode of inheritance is uncertain but evidence points towards a dominant gene. A joint
BVA/KC control scheme is in operation.

There are several other eye conditions which have an
hereditary basis and for which there are control schemes in
operation. Further information will be obtained on consulting
your veterinary surgeon.

Hip Dysplasia. This causes lameness due to partial or complete dislocation of the hip joint. It is multi-factorial, heredity
playing a part. The socket of the hip becomes shallower and
the head of the femur or thigh bone flattens so there is no close
fit between the two. Sometimes the joint luxates with the head
of the femur slipping out of the socket completely. Dogs of

many, especially the larger, breeds can be affected and clinically affected puppies have difficulty in getting up and when they move have a distinctive rolling gait. In order to assist breeders in the selection of the most suitable stock, there is a joint British Veterinary Association/Kennel Club scheme. The dog is radiographed by the owner's veterinary surgeon with the Kennel Club registration number photographed on to the plate. On payment of an extra fee this radiograph is examined by a special panel of veterinary surgeons and is appropriately scored, each hip being awarded a maximum of 26 points, according to the faults present. The lower the number the better the hips and in essence, mates should be chosen with a lower score wherever possible. In this way the condition if not eliminated will at least be controlled in the future.

House Training

No chapter on puppy management would be complete without a section on house training. The big breeder, buying a puppy for show or future breeding, may not pay much attention to this point. The smaller breeder, and the pet owner, will welcome this start to his puppy's education. Habits, both good and bad, are formed in the young with great speed, and once formed are difficult to break. It is wise, therefore, to form good habits in a puppy at an early age.

In very young puppies defecation and urination are automatic reflexes and occur after each feed. The entry of food into the stomach stimulates that unconscious rhythmic contraction of the bowel called peristalsis, and this contraction results in the passage along the bowel of the products of digestion, and their expulsion from the anus. Nothing can or should be done to interfere with this reflex action, a knowledge of it can be used as the basis for house training.

In the early days of life puppies perform these functions in the nest, and the bitch ensures cleanliness by licking up all that is passed. As soon as they are out of the nest, and having 'meals' in addition to their mother's milk, feeds should be given out of doors whenever possible. If not, and feeding has to be inside, puppies should be put out immediately after a feed, before they have time to soil the floor of their house. This routine will begin house training. A heap of sawdust or newspaper in several layers is useful in the kennel, and puppies can be trained to use it when outside conditions are impossible. When the puppy takes up its abode in the house, a tray of sawdust can still be used at night, for no young puppy can be expected to stay dry throughout an entire night.

The smell of urine is a great stimulus to repeating the performance. The anticipation and prevention of any accident in the house is therefore important. No puppy should be expected to go for several hours without relieving itself; it must not be shut in too long, or an accident is inevitable, and weeks of patient training will receive a setback. The avoidance of even one such accident is vital and puppies should be put out after every meal, first thing in the morning, last thing at night, and at frequent intervals during the day. Furthermore, young puppies should not be just put out and left; the owner should stay with them until they have relieved themselves, however tedious this may be, and then immediately let them in again. The fact that they are restored to favour, as it were, as soon as they have relieved themselves and done what was required will help to establish a ready response to this routine.

No punishment should be inflicted for lapses in house cleanness, nor indeed in any training as far as puppies are concerned. Normal puppies are quick to learn and anxious to please, and the owner should ask himself whether the lapse is not his own fault. A mild scolding is all that is really necessary, but the fact that it is out of favour is punishment enough for a normal puppy, and friendly relations should be restored as soon as possible. Praise should always be given when the puppy behaves as it should, patience on the part of the owner, coupled always with firmness, consistence and, most of all, affection, are the qualities most needed. Most puppies are easily house trained, some hardly need specific house training, habits of cleanliness seem to be inborn. Some puppies are slower to learn than others and there are a few which seem impossible to house train; for these kennel life seems the only thing. It must be said, however, that in the majority of cases, the fault is that of the owner rather than of the puppy. Most dogs are, in this respect as in others, exactly what their owners make them.

One final point should be mentioned. The young puppy has not perfect control over its bladder, and, when excited or frightened, may, without intention, pass water. This is not within the puppy's control and he should not be scolded. The condition invariably disappears with puppyhood, and owners need not feel worried.

Registration by the Kennel Club

Registration of dogs by the Kennel Club is a matter which concerns all breeders of pedigree stock. Registers of breeds, and of varieties within a breed, are kept by the Kennel Club, as well as registers of crosses within a few individual breeds, specified interbred dogs and 'any other breed', the latter term including the comparatively few and rare breeds not numerically strong enough for individual registers.

Registrations are divided into two main stages in the Kennel Club Registration System:

(a)   Recording the litter. The total number of puppies must be declared at the time of recording the litter.
(b)   Registration of individual puppies in the litter which must be carried out if they are to be shown, exported etc.

Both sire and dam must be in the active register and their owners shown in the Kennel Club records.

The signature of the sire's owner is necessary for the litter recording.

Prefixes and Affixes

An affix is a kennel name, and may be registered with the Kennel Club provided it is approved by the Committee. This affix (which should not exceed twelve letters) becomes the trademark—the hallmark, as one might almost call it—of the holder.

When the holder of a registered affix wishes to register a dog, the affix must appear as a prefix, that is the first word in the name. The dog must be (a) bred by him/her or (b) bred from parents each of which was bred by him/her. Otherwise, it must be used as a suffix, that is, the last word in the name.

Once a dog has left the breeder's ownership his/her affix may not be used in naming the dog in the future. A name already used to register a dog may be used again to register another dog of the same breed provided ten years after 1 January 1978 have elapsed since the last registration, but if that name has been entered in the Kennel Club Stud Book, it cannot ever be used again as the registered name of a dog of the same breed.

The value of a prefix, apart from its convenience to the holder, depends entirely on the stock with which it is associated. A famous prefix may be a hallmark throughout the world of the quality of its stock and the integrity of its holder. An unknown prefix may mean little or nothing until such time as its holder becomes known for his integrity and his good stock.

Change of name

The name of a dog may be changed once only in its life-time, the only change permitted is the addition of the owner's registered affix to the original registered name. The new name must not be used until the Change of Name certificate has been issued. The name of a dog cannot be changed after thirty days have elapsed from the date of the first win which qualifies it or any of its progeny for entry in the Kennel Club Stud Book.

Endorsements

The owner of a dog may request the Kennel Club to place any or all of the following endorsements on its records of the dog and to mark the relevant Registration and/or Transfer Certificates.

(a) Not eligible for entry at Shows, Field Trials, Obedience Classes and Working Trials held under Kennel Club rules.

(b) Progeny not eligible for registration.

(c) Not eligible for the issue of an export pedigree.

(d) Name unchangeable (On payment of the appropriate fee).

Any endorsement can only be lifted at the written request of the individual imposing it.

7

Hazards of Puppyhood

This book would not be complete without mention of some of the troubles which affect young puppies. The conditions are by no means confined to youngsters, far from it, but resistance at an early age may be slight, and young things react more quickly and more violently to the onset of illness than do older individuals. The list is not comprehensive but includes some of the normal risks of puppyhood.

The golden rule is to secure veterinary help at the first sign of trouble, and in order to detect such signs constant observation is needed. Early diagnosis is vitally important in treating any illness or accident, especially in the young animal, where resistance may break down quickly and a dangerous condition develop with little warning. Correct diagnosis must necessarily precede correct treatment, and this is by no means always easy, even to those with years of professional training and experience behind them. The breeder's part is to observe carefully, to notice any departure from the normal and to write down his observations, which should include a record of temperature and pulse rate. He should not administer various remedies on the hit-or-miss principle, he should call in veterinary help without delay, and his careful notes will be invaluable to the expert, who must depend on the owner for any history of the case.

It is far wiser to call in professional help for complaints which may turn out to be trifling than to fail to call it in in cases which turn out to be serious. Only the event will prove which these are, and by then it may be too late, for serious and killing diseases and slight complaints may begin with exactly the same signs.

Parasites

Parasites may be divided into internal and external.

The main external parasites are fleas, lice, ticks, harvest mites and the two forms of mange, sarcoptic (or scabies) and demodectic (follicular) mange, ringworm and cheyletiella (walking dandruff).

Fleas in numbers should not be found in any well-managed kennel, though the odd flea may appear, picked up from another dog or from grass or some other species, fowls for instance.

Dog fleas are considerably larger than human fleas, and not so active, they walk instead of hopping, and are thus easier to catch. A steel dog comb moistened with surgical or methylated spirit is useful and will remove fleas which can then be burnt. The coat should be well dusted with a suitable powder. Several are available; those containing pybuthrin are safe, even for tiny puppies. Fleas lay their eggs in cracks in wood or brick-work, and kennels or wooden beds should be thoroughly cleaned and disinfected, and all bedding burnt.

Fleas must be got rid of, they are not only irritating, and lead to constant scratching and the resulting infection of the skin, but they are one of the hosts of the tapeworm, and the source of most of these parasites which are found in dogs.

Lice occur normally only in badly nourished puppies and in dirty kennels. They are especially serious in puppies for they live on the blood of their hosts, laying their eggs on the hairs, firmly attached by a kind of cement. These eggs, nits, as they are called, must be destroyed as well as the lice themselves. Special baths and also aerosol sprays obtainable from your veterinary surgeon will control the problem. Scrupulous cleanliness throughout a kennel, a good standard of health and condition will ensure freedom from lice. The curious old idea, still not entirely abandoned, that lice can occur on a dog by spontaneous generation is entirely without foundation. Lice arise from the eggs of lice, and in their turn produce another generation of eggs, and so the generations continue.

Ticks.   Dog ticks are greyish oval, and about half an inch long, becoming rounded and swollen after a meal. They attach themselves to the skin by pincers, and feed on the blood. Easily seen in smooth-coated dogs, they must be looked for in dogs with heavy coats. They should not be pulled off, for they leave their pincers behind them, which leads to a suppurating sore. If cotton wool, moistened with surgical spirit or even methylated spirit, is held over the tick for about half a minute, it can be quickly pulled off without leaving the mouth parts behind. It should then be burned. Ticks can occur both in country areas (sheep ticks) and also in town dogs when their natural host is often found to be the hedgehog.

Harvest Mites   are tiny red crab-like insects, barely visible to the naked eye, and common in July, August and September. They occur naturally on grass and growing crops and are larval forms of another insect. They also infect human beings and intense irritation is caused both to dog and man. Areas in dogs which have little hair, and in which two skin surfaces touch, are most affected, and owing to the constant chewing and nibbling which goes on, a secondary infection may occur and cause trouble.

Powdered sulphur, dusted lightly on the parts, is a good old-fashioned preventive, but it must not be overdone, or a harvester rash may be exchanged for a sulphur rash.

Cheyletiella   the fur mite. This is a surface mite and produces excessive shedding of superficial skin scales, 'dandruff', in puppies, together with irritation along the body from head to rump. The mites can be contagious to man. Modern antiparasitic sprays and baths quickly overcome the problem.

Mange.   Other and more serious skin parasites are Scabies (sarcoptic mange), and Demodectic (follicular) mange.

The same parasite causes scabies in dog and man, and it is contagious from either to the other. It is intensely irritating and the dog scratches incessantly, making sores which usually become septic from constant biting and nibbling. The parasite burrows under the skin surface.

Demodectic mange is caused by a parasite living in the hair follicles. It is not highly contagious but, if untreated, spreads and causes destruction of skin over a wide area. It is difficult to treat locally because the parasite lies deep in the skin. Modern remedies are a great advance on those of the past, when demodectic mange was considered more or less incurable. The disease appears today to be due to an immune deficiency.

Ringworm. A fungus condition of skin which often affects puppies; small round bald areas of skin appear, with perhaps some broken hairs, and these tend to spread. Again modern remedies are more reliable than the older ones.

Treatment of all skin diseases is the province of the veterinary surgeon.

Any puppies which scratch persistently and show patches of skin with broken hair and inflammation, and any which have a strong mousy smell should have veterinary attention at once.

Internal Parasites. Among the internal parasites intestinal worms are the most common, and the usual types causing infestation in this country are the roundworm and the tapeworm.

The Roundworm. Pinkish grey in colour and three–six inches long, the roundworm is known by every breeder. There are actually two similar worms that can infect dogs, but one, Toxocara canis, is more important since it can occasionally infect other species, and has been known to cause problems in children. Apart from their own wellbeing, it is therefore important to ensure that all puppies are carefully wormed before they go to new homes. Roundworms, unlike tapeworms, pass their entire life in one host and do not require a second-ary species to complete their development. Eggs passed out in the faeces are one means by which infection is spread; these eggs, once on the ground, are very resistant and not easily killed by disinfectants. The eggs, which are invisible to the naked eye, reinfect the dog by being eaten. They hatch in the bowel and then undergo extensive migration through the tissues of the body, where they can encyst for long periods. This is known as somatic migration.

In the pregnant animal the larvae can become reactivated and pass across the placenta into the unborn puppy, where they migrate to the lungs. In puppies under five weeks of age, tracheal migration then takes place, where the larvae migrate up the windpipe, are then swallowed and develop into adult worms in the puppies' intestines. Thus puppies, by the time they are three weeks old, can be passing infected eggs. This prenatal method of infection accounts for the high proportion of young puppies that harbour worms, often despite the fact that the dam has been repeatedly wormed herself. However, even modern worm remedies can only eliminate adult worms from the bowel but one preparation 'Panacur' (Hoechst) is now claimed to kill larvae as well although daily dosing over a 3–4 week period is necessary and the preparation is expensive.

In the very young puppy the larvae migrating through the lungs can cause coughing and a nasal discharge. Once worms are present in the bowel, signs of colic become apparent, often with diarrhoea, and very soon the puppy assumes the classical pot-bellied appearance. Mucous membranes are anaemic, pale in colour, and almost glassy in appearance. Worming shoud be commenced when the puppy is about three weeks old and should be repeated at weekly intervals until the puppies leave the bitch, in order that all adult worms can, as far as possible, be eliminated. After, worming should be at eight and twelve weeks and subsequently as advised by the veterinary surgeon.

Accurate dosage is essential, especially in the very tiny puppies, where overdosage is not uncommon. It is therefore worthwhile consulting a veterinary surgeon rather than using any of the products on free sale, effective though they may be. It is natural for the bitch to clean up after her puppies while suckling. Therefore she, too, should be wormed at the same time as the puppies and should, as far as possible, be separated from them for a few hours while worming is in progress in order to cut down cross infection. Puppies are often dosed with piperazine compounds which are particularly safe, but these are usually marketed as tablets which are difficult to fractionate for very small puppies. However, Antepar syrup marketed in the Wellcome Medical range can be accurately diluted with water in order to achieve a dose rate of 100 mg/kg. Also there are specifically designed puppy wormers available today which ensure accurate dosing. If in doubt, however, a veterinary surgeon should be consulted. When actually worming, care should be taken to separate or mark puppies as each one is dosed to ensure that none is missed or doubly dosed. In order to facilitate clearing up, it is useful to rear puppies on concrete rather than grass and to make sure that all faeces are burned. Care should be taken to wash hands thoroughly after handling any faeces.

Nothing creates such a bad impression as a wormy puppy being sold, but, in view of the complexity of the method of development of worms, this can occur from time to time. However, once the purchaser understands a little of the life-cycle of the worm and appreciates the facts that worming only eliminates adults from the puppy's bowel and that repeated worming is essential, little criticism can reflect on the breeder.

The Tapeworm.   Tapeworms are more uncommon in puppies, although they can cause trouble, particularly in the smaller breeds. To complete its life cycle, the tapeworm requires an intermediate host which can be as diverse as the rabbit, in the case of hunting dogs, or fleas and lice. Thus to eradicate tapeworm completely from a kennel, not only have the inmates got to be wormed, but care has to be taken to ensure that fleas and lice are totally eradicated and that no uncooked rabbit meat is eaten.

The tapeworm attaches itself to the intestinal wall by means of a series of hooks attached around its head and it really consists of a series of individual segments which are more developed the further they are from the head. As they mature segments detach and pass out with the faeces. In an infected animal, dried segments looking like grains of rice, can often be seen sticking to the anus. Once outside the body the segments disintegrate and release the eggs which are in turn swallowed by the intermediate host, where they develop into a cyst which contains the head of a new tapeworm. When any such cysts are eaten by a dog, either by swallowing a flea or louse or by eating infected meat, the new tapeworm will start to develop—and so the lifecycle is completed.

Although tapeworm remedies are available on free sale, treatment, particularly in the case of a puppy, should be from a veterinary surgeon. Today there are several sophisticated drugs available that are well tolerated and require no purging. Some are broad spectrum and cover both roundworms and tapeworms and even other less common types of worms as well.

Diarrhoea

The term denotes the frequent passage of loose and watery motions. It is a symptom of intestinal irritation which hurries the bowel contents along before the normal absorption of fluid has taken place. Irritation may cause the bowel lining to secrete a jelly-like mucus which will be passed with the faeces.

Diarrhoea is thus rather a symptom than a disease in itself.

An acute attack of this trouble in young puppies calls for immediate consultation with the veterinary surgeon; the cause must be discovered if possible, or at any rate some causes must be eliminated. Irritant poison is unlikely in any well-managed kennel, but it is always wise to have an unbreakable rule which keeps dangerous drugs or other substances, disinfectants for instance, entirely out of the reach of any dog, and, where house dogs are concerned, human medicines must be equally inaccessible.

Virus diseases, particuarly canine parvovirus disease but also other infections may also cause acute diarrhoea. Such cases will usually include raised temperature and increased pulse rate among the signs, with possible tonsillitis. The dog's pulse is normally somewhat irregular in its beat. It may best be taken by feeling the femoral artery, the great artery of the leg, inside the thigh, at a point halfway along the femur and immediately behind it.

Worms are perhaps the most common cause of a less acute type of this trouble in puppies, and it may also be due to unsuitabe feeding or contaminated food. Raw knacker's meat may contain drugs with which a sick beast may have been drenched before its death or slaughter. Such objects as stones, cinders and other comletely unsuitable things seem to have an irresistible attraction for puppies and may cause diarrhoea or even obstruction.

A practical point here is that finesse is needed to get any such object out of the puppy's mouth, for the immediate inclination is to retain the cherished possession by swallowing it. The offer of a titbit or another toy in exchange is the best approach.

Rest is needed in any form of severe diarrhoea. Activity increases the muscular action of the bowel which drives the products of digestion along the passage. Warmth is also required.

The object of drugs is to check this action, and thereby slow the passage of food, so that water can be absorbed into the tissues. In mild cases a preparation of charcoal and kaolin is effective in soothing any inflammation of the bowel lining and absorbing any toxins present. It is worthwhile obtaining from your veterinary surgeon a simple anti-diarrhoea remedy to have as a standby.

It is necessary to check severe diarrhoea, whatever the cause, first being sure that any toxic substances have been eliminated. The loss of fluid leads to rapid dehydration, especially in young animals, with possible serious consequences.

A veterinary surgeon should be called in to deal with any cases of diarrhoea which do not clear up quickly and completely with simple remedies. Small quantities of glucose and water or better still, some of the modern ion replacement solutions which can be obtained from your veterinary surgeon should be given frequently. These prevent dehydration.

Constipation

The difficult or infrequent passage of food residue from the lower bowel is called constipation. Bowel action depends on the tone of the intestinal muscles, which cause the bowel to contract. Anything which interferes with this contraction may cause constipation. Evacuation is a reflex action in young puppies, depending on the stimulus of food entering the stomach, and this happens after every meal, though a less frequent rhythm is established as the animal grows. Constipation may be the result of a low food intake, either in illness or through under-feeding, it may be due to unsuitable diet with an inadequate residue, or muscular weakness from debility or lack of exercise.

The acute constipation occurring in certain surgical emergencies presents quite another picture. It is commonly caused by some form of obstruction of the bowel. A blockage due to something swallowed which cannot pass through the gut or to the condition called intussusception is probably the most usual form of obstruction in puppies. The signs of both are dramatic; acute pain, vomiting, lack of all bowel action often following on a little bloodstained diarrhoea. A surgical emergency of the first magnitude, it calls for immediate diagnosis and treatment.

Simple constipation in puppies should be treated first by attention to diet, with adequate fat, enough roughage in the shape of wholemeal biscuit or cereal, and plenty of water to drink as well as milk. Malt extract is pleasant and can be given in combination with cod-liver oil. Liquid paraffin may be used in teaspoonful doses, but it should not be continued for too long, on account of its Vitamin D absorbing properties.

Opportunities for play and exercise are needed, to strengthen the muscles, internal as well as external, and opportunities for regular evacuations must be ample, for a puppy is quickly house trained, and once this has happened it should never be shut in for long periods without a chance of relieving itself.

Regular doses of purgatives are most emphatically not recommended, and the use of castor oil in constipation is likely to defeat its own ends, for though a single dose is useful to get rid of anything unwholesome in the bowel, repeated doses are astringent in their effects. Constipation in puppies should be treated by the gentlest means.

Rickets

This is a deficiency disease due to lack of Vitamin D and an imbalance of calcium and phosphorus. It is rarely seen today except in badly reared puppies such as one occasionally sees from trader kennels. Other bone growth problems or osteodystrophies as they are called have, in the past, been incorrectly diagnosed as Rickets.

Fits

These arise from disturbances of the brain and may be due to many causes, including toxic conditions of all kinds (especially kidney disease), as well as to true epilepsy and to certain hereditary conditions. A fit may be so mild that it goes almost unnoticed or may be a violent convulsive seizure with loss of consciousness and often involuntary defaecation and urination. Sometimes an animal may come out of one fit and immediately go into another. This is a conditon known as status epilepticus and is considerably more serious than the odd isolated fit. There are some breeders who regard fits as almost normal in the young puppy, and it is true that in the very young, be it baby or puppy, the nervous system is much more sensitive than it is in the adult. Consequently stimulae which would go unnoticed in later life are sufficient to produce the chaotic cerebral disturbance that we call a fit. Nevertheless in the healthy puppy, fits should not occur except on isolated occasions; then they should be a matter for concern and full veterinary investigation.

The main stimulae that cause fits in puppies are difficulties or pain in cutting teeth, irritation of the bowel from worms, gastric upsets, colic, or even just plain over-eating. Highly nervous animals that become over-excited or have an elevated temperature may also end up convulsing. However, if feeding and general management are satisfactory, irrespective of the breed, even the slightest suspicion of a fit should be discussed at once with the veterinary surgeon. The old maximum of 'better safe than sorry' is a very good principle to follow.

When a puppy is in a fit, the best first-aid measures are quiet and darkness, with the less handlng the better. Remember that during a convulsion the puppy is often unconscious and that, when the fit is over, for a variable time it may not be able to see or hear properly. Therefore the stimulus of trying to comfort the animal may have just the reverse effect and send the animal into further convulsive episodes; the more fits the puppy has the greater the chance of status epilepticus, which should be avoided at all costs. Although very distressing to the onlooker, it should be remembered that, when the puppy is thrashing around in a fit, he seldom hurts himself and that trying to hold him down to prevent him from moving sometimes has the reverse effect, making him even more agitated. Thus while the puppy is in a fit, he should be left strictly alone, although it is obviously advantageous if he could be placed on a carpet or soft bed. Bigger animals should be left alone in a darkened, quiet room and any small moveable furniture which could be knocked over and cause injury should be quietly removed. On recovery, the animal will appear dazed and is often covered in saliva or faeces and urine. Attempts to clean up should be delayed until the dog is fully conscious— otherwise there is again the possibility of sending him into another fit.

Once he has settled down, veterinary advice should be sought as soon as possible since delay, as with so many other conditions involving young animals, can prove disastrous.

Virus Diseases

A virus is a parasite of plant or animal life. It is a filter-passing organism and can be seen only with an electron microscope. Unlike bacteria, viruses can only reproduce themselves within the cells of their host. Virus diseases are infectious. Modern research has shown that viruses often exist in groups or complexes, the members of which are related to each other but differ in their actions and effects. A virus complex should not be taken to mean a number of viruses which have similar actions. Different viruses can sometimes have exactly the same effects. This theory accounts for the failure of immunization which can occur as immunization is specific against a particular organism.

We see this virus complex in human influenza, of which there are several types causing illness differing in many respects. It would seem likely that as any population, human or canine, becomes immune to any infection either by contracting the infection and recovering from it, or by means of successful inoculation against the disease, an immune population is gradually built up. Rather than the disease being totally eradicated—as has happened, for example, with smallpox—sometimes the virus gradually changes its type or an already existing alternative type comes to the fore, because the change of environment has deprived the original virus of its means of existence.

This is what is thought to have occurred with hard pad disease and distemper, which are now considered to be slightly differing forms of the same disease, caused by the same virus complex.

Distemper.   Immediately post war, there were widespread epidemics of distemper or its hard pad variant and the immunity resulting in the animals that survived, together with the widespread use of vaccination, has reduced the incidence of the virus. However there are still sporadic and localized outbreaks. It is possible, in future, that further outbreaks may occur, due to other variants, or mutants of the virus as they are called. Recently distemper has become once more relatively common due to the lack of regular boosting that has taken place due to economic and other reasons in certain parts of the country. No vaccine, animal or human, can be guaranteed to give 100% of permanent protection. Therefore, despite the fact that the incidence of the natural disease may be low, it is essential to follow the local veterinary surgeon's recommendation regarding the reinforcing or booster doses, since these may well vary, area to area.

Additional factors that will affect the timing of boosters are show and breeding programmes, holidays, whether the dog is being taken into a new area or being taken into boarding kennels, etc. This is the reason why, when breeders compare notes, advice from individual veterinary surgeons appears to be superficially divergent or sometimes conflicting. It should be remembered that distemper can affect dogs of all ages.

Basically, the symptoms may be of two forms: catarrhal or nervous. In the catarrhal form, the dog may have a high temperature, runny eyes and nose, a cough and sometimes diarrhoea. Nervous signs are more serious and often follow the catarrhal form although, particularly in dogs that have some partial immunity (as occurs in those that have been inoculated but have not had regular boosters) nervous signs can be the first indication of any trouble. They can take the form of fits, a kind of nervous twitch known as chorea, or paralysis. Recent work has shown that nervous signs can sometimes occur months, or even years, after the initial infection. Infected animals may also show hardening of the pads and sometimes the nose. Infection is usually spread by the virus on droplets of moisture. Dogs may pick it up by sniffing where other dogs have been. Thus it is sensible to keep your dog away from other animals and prevent it from going to places where other dogs exercise, certainly until it has got a solid immunity from vaccination. It is for this reason that puppies should be isolated until after they have been vaccinated.

Contagious Virus Hepatitis. This is another major virus disease of dogs and was originally described by Rubarth in Sweden in 1947. It is very contagious and in its acute form can prove fatal within twenty-four hours, often without any signs being shown by the animal—thus allowing no time for the veterinary surgeon to treat the animal. It is now known that, apart from the acute form, the disease can affect dogs in several different ways. The virus can cause damage to the liver, the kidneys and the eyes; sometimes it may be responsible for a respiratory infection. The disease is also one of the factors concerned with the so-called 'fading puppy' syndrome, which can result in the death of very young puppies.

These varying disease patterns are probably a reflection of the different routes whereby this virus can infect, together with a varying susceptibility of different dogs to infection and perhaps with a difference in the virulence of the infecting organism. Obviously, the best line of defence is prevention, which can be achieved very effectively by vaccination. The vaccine, together with that for the *Leptospiral* diseases, considered next, is usually incorporated with the distemper vaccine.

Leptospiral Disease. Dogs can be infected by two Leptospira organisms, which are bacteria and not viruses. One, *Leptospira Icterhaemorrhagae*, is an organism carried by rats and one which can also be passed on to man. It causes Leptospiral jaundice, known as Weils disease in human medicine. Since it is transmitted by rats the disease is particularly prevalent among dogs on farms, at ports, and in mining areas. Infected dogs usually develop jaundice as a result of damage to the liver by the bacteria. Haemorrhages in the mucous membranes of the body can also occur; these result in very dark faeces which are due to the bleeding into the bowel. Prolonged treatment and nursing are necessary but, despite these, many dogs can die. Therefore, prophyllactic inoculations are sensible—and of course rats should be eliminated from the neighbourhood of all kennels.

Canicola Fever, due to Leptospira Canicola, is also a disease which can affect man. Although it can be immediately fatal, the disease usually runs a very much more chronic course in the dog and can be responsible for a high proportion of deaths later in life because of damage to the kidneys. The disease is spread by bacteria in the urine, so lampposts are a serious source of infection in towns. One survey has shown that about 50% of town dogs have evidence of past infection. Vaccination is again particularly effective and it is for this reason that the two Leptospiral bacterial diseases are combined with the two viral diseases in the so-called quadrivalent vaccination programme.

Parvovirus Infection. Canine Parvovirus Disease first occurred in the United Kingdom in 1978 and assumed epidemic proportions during the summer of 1982. It is caused by a virus very similar to that which causes Feline Enteritis in the cat. Originally it could take one of two forms: (a) the myocardial form causing heart disease in very young puppies. As more and more bitches acquired a natural or vaccinal immunity to the disease which they confer to their offspring in the womb and via the milk, parvovirus myocarditis is rarely seen today. Much more important is (b) the enteric form, characterised by evil-smelling bloody diarrhoea. This can occur in puppies of all ages up to nine months of age or even older and can occur sometimes in spite of vaccination. This is because in certain individuals maternal immunity or the protection acquired from the dam can persist beyond the period when vaccination is normally carried out. Thus, when this maternal immunity wanes, since at the time of vaccination it was strong enough to negate the effects of vaccination, the puppy is left unprotected.

A lot of hard work by vaccine manufacturers has resulted in a new generation of vaccines that will now give protection in the face of a high level of maternal immunity but nevertheless repeat inoculations against canine parvovirus are still essential. Parvovirus vaccination is now incorporated into the normal puppy vaccines so that complete protection usually involves vaccination against distemper (hardpad), hepatitis (a liver disease), canine parvovirus and two forms of leptospirosis or kidney disease.

Rabies.   Rabies is a virus infection to which man and all warm-blooded animals are susceptible. It is a disease that at present we do not have, and certainly do not want, in this country. It attacks the central nervous system and causes paralysis and convulsions: in man it is invariably fatal. In humans it is usually caused by the bite from a pet that has been infected by a wild or stray animal. It is here that the danger lies, for if the disease were introduced to this country by irresponsible people smuggling in a dog from the Continent, our wildlife population (particularly foxes) could become infected and act as a reservoir for infection. Although vaccines are available which could give some protection to our pets, these would do nothing to protect the wildlife population; therefore this reservoir would continue to increase. Then, any animal bite or scratch, however slight, would be a cause for fear. No pet-owner could be completely at ease and any family picnic in the country could be fraught with danger. This country has been virtually free from rabies for over three-quarters of a century, but the disease occurs regularly in almost every part of the world and has been spreading across Europe so that today it is only about forty miles from the Channel coast. It is only our island situation that has kept us free for so long, and provided people are not irresponsible enough to smuggle animals in and disobey the present quarantine laws (which have been sufficiently effective to pick up some thirty cases since 1924) we should remain free. Unfortunately, detected illegal landings are occurring at the rate of approximately a hundred a year—

and it is these that could lead to a breakdown in the system.

Convalescence

A period of recuperation is necessary after any serious disease, and especially virus and bacterial infections. The tissues of the body, including the brain, can be severely poisoned by the toxins of disease, in animals as well as in human beings. No one who has ever had a severe attack of influenza will forget the utter debility, mental as well as physical, which follows it and which may last for some time.

Too often dog owners lack imagination and do not realize this. They expect their dog, having recovered from the worst effects of an infectious illness, to be able to resume its normal life immediately as if nothing had happened. Breeders and owners of dogs, and especially puppies, should remember the importance of 'going slow' for a time after any serious illness. Exercise should only be resumed gradually and with care; food should be good, not by increasing bulk but by additional protein and vitamins, especially A and D, and the B complex, provided by halibut-liver oil and Vetzyme in increased doses. Imagination is always needed in handling dogs, especially sick dogs, and if the owner treats a sick or convalescent dog as he would a child in similar conditions, he will not go far wrong.

Fading Puppies

This condition has been known for some time. It has been attributed to many causes, one of which, acid milk, lacks any reasonable foundation and need not be considered here. Much has been discovered about the condition in the last ten years, but more work needs to be done before a comprehensive picture of the varied causes can be presented.

The general picture of a fading litter is that of an apparently healthy bitch, giving birth to apparently healthy puppies, but this lasts for a few hours only. The affected puppies find difficulty in sucking, they get cold, perhaps a little blue about the mouth, they cry incessantly with a feeble whimper and get progressively weaker, and the bitch loses interest in them. After a day or two they gradually fade out and die. Some members of a litter may not be affected, often all are lost.

Poor management and conditions may contribute to fading out, and in this category Hodgman, the late Director of the Animal Health Trust, includes the premature tying-off of the umbilical cord, thereby depriving the puppy of a certain amount of blood which would have passed into its circulation from the placenta if it had been given time to do so; many breeders do not wait for the bitch to sever the cord herself. On the other hand the writer has noticed that many of her own bitches have divided the cord almost before the puppy is completely born. If the bitch does not herself sever the cord within a few moments after birth, the breeder should prepare to divide it himself. Before cutting, he should squeeze gently towards the puppy throughout the length of the cord from the direction of the placenta downwards, thus expressing all available blood into the puppy's circulation.

Poor feeding of the dam, bad conditions at whelping, above all cold, would seriously weaken resistance to any infection or toxic condition present in the puppies. It would appear however that in the majority of cases of fading puppies, some factor other than bad management is needed to give the typical picture.

The condition is thus multifactorial. Infections certainly play a part. The most important of these are streptococcal infections (BHS), the first organism to be investigated in connection with fading. A bitch can carry a residual infection after an attack of tonsillitis, or any other disease caused by this streptococcus. She may appear perfectly normal, but may have a history of the same trouble with previous litters. The symptoms of fading appear, and pups die rapidly if no treatment is given. Antibiotics act dramatically in many cases if given in adequate doses as soon as signs of fading appear. It should be given both to puppies and dam.

Canine Virus Hepatitis can also be implicated as can other virus diseases. Residual infection can remain in the same way after a sub-acute or even unapparent attack by the virus. Signs of fading out resemble those caused by the streptococcus.

Puppies are susceptible to attack by this virus in early infancy, and the virus itself is thought to have the power of passing the placental barrier to infect the unborn whelp.

The present view is that fading in puppies may be due to a number of factors many not yet elucidated, and that beta haemolytic streptococcus and canine virus hepatitis account for a proportion only of cases of fading puppies. Antisera are available from your veterinary surgeon.

Accidents

Though these would appear to be the greatest hazards of pup-pyhood, they can be reduced to the minimum by careful management and forethought. Most can be avoided by the establishment of a routine which quickly becomes second nature. Drugs, both canine and human, are never left within possible reach of any dog or puppy. Fire risks are made negli-gible by using only the safest kinds of appliances and installing them in the safest possible way. Domestic hazards, as when a dog which sleeps in the kitchen accidentally turns on a gas tap, are made impossible. Road accidents are avoided by training, and by the *only* certain precaution on roads which carry much traffic, and that is keeping the dog on a lead.

The unexpected accident, never considered as a possibility until it happens, is always tragic. Such a case was mentioned some years ago, when a young dog was put into its sleeping kennel wearing its collar. In the morning it was found hanged. It must have jumped up and caught its collar on a big nail in the wall. Constant forethought, and a knowledge of dogs and of the kinds of things they do, should avoid most of these par-ticular hazards of puppyhood.

8

Introducing Genetics

Every dog breeder is using genetics, whether he realizes it or not, just as the famous Monsieur Jourdain was speaking prose all his life without knowing it.

Whenever a breeder selects a mate for his bitch with a view to improving the resulting litter in one or more directions, he is putting the laws of heredity into practice.

Dog breeding is both art and science; art the product of natural aptitude (the eye for a dog); science the utilization of genetic laws whether recognized or not. Those breeders who scoff at the idea of science as a help in breeding do their best to make use of its principles by selective breeding.

However little we believe in making use of the laws of heredity to the small extent possible to us, or even in the laws themselves, we cannot get rid of them by turning our backs on them. They are just as much a part of Nature as the law of gravity or the solar system. They remain working quietly in the background, and it is impossible to escape the consequences of their activity. But we can harness them to our purpose to some extent just as we have harnessed the vast natural forces of electricity.

The breeder's choice does not lie between genetics or no genetics. There is, in fact, no choice open to us. We can try to follow natural laws to the best of our ability, or we can refuse to recognize them, but they persist, as they have since the origins of life upon the earth.

The most ardent geneticist would not, however, claim that his science was a short-cut to breeding champions or perfect dogs, even if there were agreement about what perfect dogs should be. And the main reason for this is that the breeding unit is the dog, and not the gene.

The following chapters are no textbook on genetics, which the author is in no way qualified to write. They are an attempt, by a practical breeder with an interest in heredity, to show that even an elementary knowledge of this subject can be of absorbing interest and practical help to the dog breeder, though it by no means solves all his problems.

Science is 'the attempt to arrange and classify under certain principles and laws, the various known facts about a particular branch of knowledge and so enable one to understand them'.[1] The principles and laws arrived at are at first tentative, and are continually tested and re-tested against further observation and experiment. If found to be valid, they can be assembled into an acceptable theory which provides a reasonable explanation for all observed facts. If later, new facts are discovered which invalidate the theories formed, and this is constantly happening, then the scientist must reconsider his theory, and must try to find an alternative pattern into which the new fact can be fitted. The essence of scientific study is to fit theories to facts, and never facts to theories. Selecting those facts which support a cherished theory, and leaving out of the calculation those uncomfortable facts which refute it, is the scientist's worst crime.

At this early stage the language of genetics must be mentioned. Some would call it jargon. But jargon is the language of any specialized subject, the sciences, the arts, the trades, sport and so on. And the virtue of these specialized languages is that they use in the main a single word with a precise meaning, to describe what would otherwise take a long and possibly involved sentence. This sort of writing would be both tedious to write and difficult to follow. One thing must be borne in mind in connection with any specialized language, especially that of the sciences. Words have a precise meaning, and are not used loosely in the way they so often are in the language of ordinary life, when they often mean just what the speaker intends them to mean at the moment.

The language of genetics is, of course, no exception to this rule, but as few such words as possible will be used here, and all will be explained in the glossary at the end. May I beg those readers with an interest in the subject, to learn them, for, after one explanation when first used, the correct words will be employed in these pages.

[1] *Principles of Genetics.* Sinnot and Dunn. McGraw Hill Book Co. 1939.

Genetics is the science of heredity and one of the younger of the biological sciences, which are those which study life and living substances. Gregor Mendel, an Austrian monk, is the father of this new science, though he probably did not realize this at the time his work was published in 1866. His papers remained hidden in the archives of a scientific journal in the town of Brno, in what is now Czechoslovakia, until the end of the century when they were discovered and their importance recognized by several independent observers, among them our scientist Bateson who had already come independently to some of the same conclusions.

For many years heredity had been the subject of interest and conjecture. The tendency for individuals related by descent to resemble each other, must have been recognized from the earliest times. There is little doubt that, early in the history of the human race, man, in the light of this knowledge, began to choose mates for his domestic animals, in the attempt to breed specimens more and more suitable for the work they had to perform. As selective breeding began to supersede random matings, many ideas about heredity grew up. Some were true, many had to be abandoned in the light of advancing knowledge.

The question, unanswered until Mendel made his discoveries, was exactly *how* qualities of all kinds are transmitted from parent to child, both in plants and animals—what, in fact, is the mechanism of inheritance?

The generally accepted theory of the time (the latter half of the nineteenth century), shared by Charles Darwin, the great naturalist and student of heredity of his day, was something he described as 'Blended Inheritance'—that is to say a mixing and amalgamation of ancestral characters afresh in every generation, in such a way that their identity was lost and that they could never again be separated. In such a way a custard is made, by cooking eggs and milk together. The resulting product is unlike either of its component parts, and these can never again be separated into their original form. The word 'blood' and 'bloodlines', still used by breeders, express this to some extent, but the meaning is imprecise.

Mendel's revolutionary theory, which was found to work in practice, and indeed to be the only theory which did explain known facts, was that certain particles or factors, later to be known as genes, are inherited in related pairs, one member of each pair from each parent. These factors come together in the fertilized egg cell, and act and react on each other in various ways, while retaining their own identity, and are passed on with this identity to subsequent generations, being separated in the process but not lost. Related pairs of genes have been mentioned, and 'related' in this sense means that both members of the gene pair control, or share with other pairs of genes the control of, the same character, the word used to describe a genetic characteristic, quality, or attribute. 'Character' refers to what is present in the individual as the result of gene action. Genes are not the same as characters, but are responsible for them.

This theory of Mendel's was indeed a revolutionary one, and it has superseded others because it accounts for all observed facts, and explains problems which before had found no answer.

But why, one may ask, if genes survive as entities, are not individuals of one family, whether dogs, humans or any other species, more alike than they are?

This is due to Variability, that is, the inherent capacity for change, the genetic name for which is Variation. Without Variation, there could have been no progress from primitive dog to the many breeds we see today, some ludicrously unalike. Without Variation, man could not have emerged from the primeval slime to pass through the evolutionary stages to near man, true man, primitive man, man of today, man, we hope, of tomorrow.

Variations   are due to several causes. Those due to heredity can occur only through some change in the heredity pattern of Mendelian factors we call genes, by the rearrangement of existing genes or the introduction of new ones. Genes and gene combinations can be regrouped in relation to each other during the process of cell division which occurs in the reproductive cells of the two parents, and the subsequent reunion of elements from both to form the new individual. There are gene rearrangements which increase differences between individuals and gene combinations which lessen such differences. We shall discuss them in the next chapter.

New genes, or modification of existing genes, can be brought about by the process of Mutation.

Mutation   is a sudden, usually unpredictable, and always permanent change in a hereditary factor or gene, which alters its effect, so that the organism in which the mutation occurs is different from the normal. Mutations are rare and often harmful, but they are a necessary part of evolution, for they are essential to variation, without the possibility of which adaptation to environmental changes could not occur. Mutant genes breed true in their new form and can produce profound and permanent changes in the hereditary pattern. We know that radiation is responsible for mutation. Radiation from the sun has acted on life throughout the earth's duration; man-made radiation now adds its quota to the total, and its good results must be balanced against its dangers.

Man can, of course, take a hand in bringing about variation in his domestic animals by means of selective breeding. Faults can be eliminated and virtues introduced, and this is probably the most practical aspect of the subject for livestock breeders. Careful matings within a breed can improve general quality and new breeds can be made by crossbreeding with two or more.

Environment   is another agent of variation, it is the impact on the organism of outside circumstances; such circumstances as nutrition, climate, disease and a host of others. Intra-uterine environment (the gestation period) is also included in this category. Maternal illness of various kinds can affect the unborn offspring, and malnutrition of the mother during pregnancy can seriously interfere with the nutrition of the young. But these pre-natal conditions, like events occurring after birth, do not alter the hereditary pattern and their results in the offspring are not inherited.

An example of this in dogs can be seen in tails and dew claws. Tails in some breeds have been docked for very many years but, except very rarely indeed, puppies are still born with tails. The hereditary pattern is decided in general at conception, and environment does not change it, although it may modify fulfilment of the design. Radiation is probably the only environmental circumstance which can change the genetic pattern, and this it does by causing gene mutations.

Heredity and environment are the two great forces on which development depends. Their respective functions may be roughly compared with those of architect and builder. The former responsible for the original building plan, the latter for the work of construction. If either should fail in his task the building suffers. The best builder cannot build well to a faulty plan, and the best plan can be ruined by bad workmanship. So it is with heredity and environment. The perfect hereditary pattern needs the right environment to enable it to be realized, the best environment cannot correct a faulty pattern.

Let us take an example. Strains of dogs which are normally well boned will produce puppies with the capability of forming good bone. But if the bitch is badly nourished during pregnancy and lactation and/or if the puppies are badly fed and reared, bone tissue will not develop as it should have done, and rickets may result, a disease due mainly to poor nutrition and especially to absence of Vitamin D in the diet. There may also be a hereditary tendency to rickets, though the disease may be prevented in susceptible puppies by careful treatment and correct feeding.

Thus heredity and environment can act in two different and opposite directions. In the first case, that of badly reared puppies, faulty environment prevents good hereditary design from being fulfilled. In the second case, hereditary susceptibility to rickets, a good environment prevents the development of a faulty hereditary tendency. But the environment does not correct the genetic pattern by changing any of the genes, the two patterns, good and bad, will remain unchanged, except by gene rearrangements which may occur as previously described, in reproductive cell division.

Natural Selection.   The theory of Natural Selection, first made prominent by Charles Darwin, in the latter part of the nineteenth century, has been well described as follows: 'The working of the environment on a variable population bringing about evolution in certain directions.'[1] It is the beginning of all modern views on the origin and development of man. The theory could be briefly described as the survival of the fittest, though this is an over-simplification. Its essence is that those species and individuals best adapted to their environment survive and multiply, while those ill-adapted, or not adapted at all, eventually perish. Natural selection is still at work, and a perfect present-day example of it is the behaviour of certain bacteria and viruses in face of modern medical treatment. Only those which are adapted to resist the action of antibiotics survive and continue, and as the non-resistant strains die out, the resistant strains increase and multiply and present new problems for research. We have seen that variation is necessary to change, and Darwin knew this, but in the absence of the modern knowledge of cells and how they behave, he did not know exactly how change comes about.

Genetics then is concerned with the transfer of characters from individual to individual, with the accompanying variation which is essential to it.

We know that no two individuals are exactly alike, however closely related they may be, with the exception of identical twins which are developed from a single egg cell and are therefore alike in every respect. The idea that heredity of, say litter-mates must be to all intents and purposes identical is incorrect, as we shall see later.

'Like breeds like' is an old saying often heard, and so it does, but only if outward appearance is a reflection of inherited factors, which is not quite what people mean when they quote this saying. Individuals may be alike in the outward appearance which geneticists call Phenotype, they may be alike in the hereditary pattern called Genotype, they may be alike in both to a considerable extent, but the identical twins already mentioned, the products of a single egg, are the only perfect match of two individuals.

The more closely related individuals are, the more likely they are to resemble each other both in heredity and in appearance, but it is normally a general likeness, with considerable differences in detail. We all know that members of a

[1]*Elementary Genetics.* Wilma George. Macmillan. 1956.

litter may be both alike and unalike in many of their characters. Their later breeding performances are the sole test of their genetic worth, and we shall see why later on.

We have said that the unit of breeding is the dog, and not the gene: the dog, with its innumerable genes for this that and the other character, for details of appearance and for psychological tendencies, for habits and mannerisms, and all we mean when we talk about one individual as distinct from another. Even little tricks of behaviour perhaps peculiar to a single dog, will be passed to his descendants throughout a closely bred strain.

We want our stock to pass on the favourable genes they possess, and there may be some less favourable which we should like to get rid of. We may wish to introduce new and desirable genes from other animals. We can only postulate the presence of genes by the characters which are their outward expression, and so there may be many genes present in any animal which give no indication of their existence for various reasons as we shall see in the next chapter.

Breeding dogs, therefore, will always be something of an adventure in which genetics can give us some clues. Characters are not genes, one might compare them to the clue in the crossword puzzle of which the gene is the meaning. Characters are the visible expression of genes, resulting from gene action modified by environment.

Genetics can help us elucidate the puzzle in many ways. Used wisely it can provide short cuts to improvement and in some directions certainties instead of merely hopes. Moreover, there is immense interest and even excitement in a subject which deals with life and its continuity, with the literal passing on of living tissue, a pattern in miniature, in a single minute cell, of the whole complicated structure of living beings, reaching back beyond history to the origins of life itself.

9

The Cell

The cell is the unit of life, for it contains the living substances which pass from generation to generation and which decide the hereditary pattern of the organism and also the means by which it is developed.

If we want to understand something of the processes of heredity, we must learn something of what cells are and of how they carry out their functions. No understanding of genetics, even the most rudimentary, is possible without knowing something about the cell.

It is a microscopic body, consisting of the living substance protoplasm, surrounded by its own cell membrane. It contains, as its main structural and functional unit, the nucleus, also surrounded by its membrane, the nuclear membrane. The nucleus contains the chromosomes with their genes which are the means by which the hereditary pattern is both passed on and executed.

Protoplasm within the cell is called cytoplasm, and that within the nucleus is called nucleoplasm. Both are composed of proteins and nucleic acids, varying in composition, and they play a major part in the differentiation of cells which occurs during the development of the fertilized egg (the zygote) into the complicated mature body, with its widely different types of structure and function.

We must now consider the chromosomes, so called because they are bodies which, during their active phase, can be suitably dyed. The chromosome is indistinguishable from the surrounding nucleoplasm during the resting period of the cell, but can easily be seen under the microscope when the cell becomes active as it does when preparing to divide in order to reproduce itself.

Chromosomes are condensations of nucleoplasm into elongated rod-like bodies of various sizes and shapes, on which the genes are arranged like beads on a string. Like genes, chromosomes occur in pairs, one member of each pair being derived from each parent. Similar members of a chromosome pair are homologous, the prefix 'homo' denoting like, in contrast to 'hetero' unlike.

The chromosome number is constant for every species. Man is known to have 46 (23 pairs), the dog is believed to have 78 (39 pairs), while the fruit-fly (Drosophila) has 8 (4 pairs). Owing to its simple chromosome pattern and the speed with which it reproduces itself, this fly has been used in much genetic research.

One pair of chromosomes, the sex chromosomes, differs from all the others.

Sex Chromosomes

These are specialized, in that they serve the function of reproduction, as well as transmitting hereditary factors. They carry fewer genes than those carried on the ordinary chromosomes (autosomes as they are called).

Like all other chromosomes, sex chromosomes are present in every cell in the body and there they carry out a secondary sexual function, relating to normal growth and the establishment of sexual maturity.

In the reproductive organs, or gonads, the male testicle and the female ovary, they are differentiated in such a way that they are able to divide in a particular method, as we shall see shortly.

The difference between sex chromosomes and autosomes lies in their contents, and the facts described are common to all mammals. The members of the female sex chromosome pair are similar, and labelled as XX. The male chromosome pair is dissimilar and is labelled XY. The Y chromosome is smaller and carries fewer genes than the X. It appears much less important. Females pass on an X chromosome to all their offspring. Males pass on an X chromosome to all their daughters and a Y chromosome to all their sons.

The number of X chromosomes seems to determine potential sex, in that XX = female, and XY = male, not so much by the presence of Y as by the absence of double X. However,

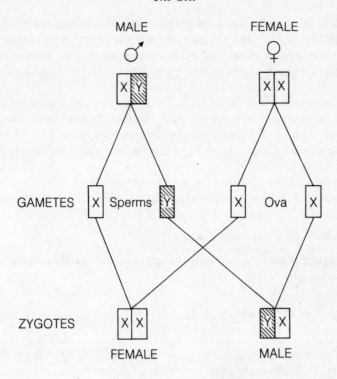

Figure 1

SEX DETERMINATION

Distribution of X and Y chromosomes

genes in each chromosome also exercise a sex-determining influence, in the one case suppressing maleness in the female zygote, and in the other femaleness in the male.

It is easy to see how such actions might be hampered or modified to produce abnormalities of structure or function in the reproductive system. As far as the author knows, no such effects have been investigated in canine genetics, but that certain patterns of sexual behaviour are shared by both sexes is obvious from the reaction of bitches in season to other bitches. Masculine instincts have not been entirely suppressed.

Recent work in human genetics has, in fact, proved that chromosome aberrations occur; in some cases three chromosomes can be present instead of two, in others one is missing. These conditions are known to give rise to physical and mental defects and to intermediate sexual types.

The Y chromosome plays a minor part in heredity, and the X chromosome is clearly not strictly differentiated as male or female, for it is constantly shuffled across from one to the other sex, and elements for both sexes are present in the early stages of the zygote.

Normally, sexual development is straightforward, but gene action in one direction or the other is the deciding factor.

The Mechanism of Reproduction

In higher plants and animals life reproduces itself by cell division, of which there are two kinds:

1. Simple Cell Division or Mitosis

This is ordinary cell division which is responsible for growth and formation of all the organs of the body. When the cell is ready to divide the wall of the nucleus dissolves away releasing chromosomes into the cell. These appear jumbled up at first but quickly align themselves in a pre-ordered fashion across the centre of the cell. They then each split into two. Each half then travels to opposite ends of the cell whence a membrane forms around each group, thus forming two new nucleii. The cell itself then splits forming two daughter cells. Each cell in the dog contains 78 chromosomes (39 pairs) and each chromosome behaves in this way during mitosis. It is by this means that a single cell develops into a mass of cells which compose the organism. These in turn become specialised and thus muscle cells, nerve cells and skin cells are finally formed.

2. Sexual Reproduction or meiosis

This is the form of cell division which takes place in the gonads or sex organs preparatory to sexual reproduction. It occurs in the sex cells of both partners and ensures that at fertilisation chromosome numbers are not continually doubled up. Again the nuclear membrane disappears and the chromosomes line up in an orderly fashion across the centre of the cell. However instead of splitting they come together in pairs thus in the dog there are 39 pairs. Each chromosome splits longitudinally into two chromatids parts of which 'cross over' with the other chromatids of the pair. This is 'crossing over', the main agent in variation. After crossing over has occurred the cell divides into two daughter cells, very much as occurs in mitosis. However daughter cells now only contain half the chromosome number (39). Fertilisation when male and female cells join once more restores the chromosome number and the resulting fertilised egg or zygote then begins to divide by the process of mitosis already described.

It is an arresting thought that this single cell, this zygote, is the only physical link between the generations, the only piece of living substance which links them together, from the time life first appeared on the earth. It carries with it the past and the future, and it links every generation with all those before and after.

The processes of mitosis and meiosis can be studied under the microscope, and chromosome actions observed: chromosome maps have been made from the simpler organisms, notably the fruit-fly.

The manner in which chromosomes and genes meet and react to form a new individual is the subject of the next chapter.

This meeting-place could be called the cross-roads of heredity, for, at this point many paths meet and diverge, and many changes of direction are possible. Pure chance dictates most of these, but conscious design can play a part if directed with knowledge by the breeder.

This meeting-place, as one writer has happily put it, is the place 'where genes are shuffled and dealt'.[1]

---

[1] *Genetics.* Kalmus. Penguin Books. 1943.

10

Chromosomes and Genes

Mendel's work must now be considered more closely. His theories were revolutionary. The factors he discovered and the ways in which he interpreted them are the foundations of the science of genetics.

Mendel worked inductively, that is from the particular to the general. His published work was an investigation of some seven opposed characters he noticed in garden peas, such characteristics as red and white flowers, round and wrinkled seeds, green and yellow seeds and tall and short plants. He studied these pairs at first singly, then in combinations of two and three, tracing them through many generations, and making accurate and extensive notes which included counting of large numbers of results.

He was fortunate in that the characters he chose for investigation happened to be those controlled by a single pair of factors (genes as we now know them), and that these genes happened to be in the relation to each other which Mendel discovered and called dominant and recessive. He had also established a strain of pure-breeding peas. The word 'pure' in this sense implies genetic purity, namely the possession of identical genes in the pair responsible for any given character. And since the colour of his pea flowers was one of Mendel's studies, let us bring 'genetic purity' from the general to the particular, and state that his red pea flowers carried no gene for any colour but red, and his white no gene for any colour but white.

Mendel knew nothing of genes or chromosomes, but in order to account for his theories he had to postulate the presence of 'factors, or particles', responsible for the transmission of inheritance. Long after his death, when a new branch of biology, the study of cell structure and behaviour called cytology, had led to renewed interest in the subject of heredity, the existence of chromosomes was established, and they provided the perfect vehicle for the transmission of Mendel's factors.

At this stage it will be helpful to mention the way in which generations are described genetically, a logical sequence and easy to remember. Mendel's original pair of peas (both it will be remembered pure-breeding) are called 'the First Parental Generation', P.1 for short. The parents of P.1 are P.2 and so on. The offspring of P.1 are called 'the First Filial Generation', F.1 for short, their own offspring F.2 and so on. Mendel then went on to breed his pure red peas to his pure white and the resulting plants formed the F.1 generation. They were all red, in spite of one white parent.

What had happened to the colour white? We know that every individual resulting from crossing two opposed pure-breeding characters must carry one gene for each. Clearly the red had supressed the white, and the flowers were no longer pure-breeding as regards colour, they were, in fact, hybrids. This word has a specialized meaning in genetics. A hybrid character is one which results from the coming together of a dissimilar pair of genes, it is the opposite of genetic purity. Red predominated in this F.1 generation, and completely masked white, and Mendel gave the name dominant to the gene for red in his pea flowers, and to all other genes which behave in the same way. White had disappeared and he called it recessive. This disappearance, as we shall see, was temporary, the gene for white was masked, but still maintained its own identity. This pair of genes are called alleles or allelomorphs.

We can now define the terms dominant and recessive:

Dominant Genes are those which have the property of suppressing the effects of their partners in the gene pair, which are said to be heterozygous. It follows that a character due to a dominant gene manifests itself when present in single dose only, that is inherited from one parent only.

Recessive Genes on the other hand are masked by their dominant partners unless inherited in double dose, that is from both parents, and are homozygous.

There could be no clearer indication that the breeding worth of any animal cannot be judged on appearance alone.

The accepted method of indicating dominant and recessive

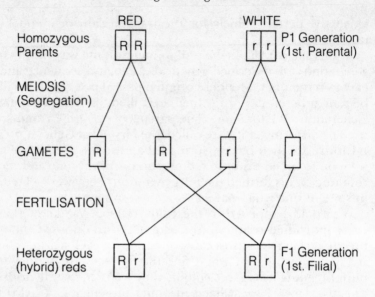

Figure 2

THE MATING OF TWO DISSIMILAR HOMOZYGOTES

genes on paper is to use the two forms of an appropriate letter of the alphabet, the capital for the dominant gene, the small letter for the recessive. In the absence of dominance, the capital is used for the normal.

On the previous page the words *homozygous* and *heterozygous* were introduced. These are among the most important terms in genetics. The members of a dissimilar gene pair are called heterozygous. Our P.1 gene pairs were both homozygous, the F.1 offspring were all heterozygous.

The next stage in Mendel's experiment was to cross the members of F.1, all hybrids, that is impure for both red and white.

It would be interesting to know whether Mendel realized how epoch-making his discovery was when this generation, F.2, showed the reappearance of white flowers in the average proportions of three red flowers to one white. But, and this is important from the breeder's point of view, only one red was pure-breeding, the double dominant. The remaining two reds were hybrids, with one gene for red and one for white, the recessive white being masked by the single dominant gene for red. The fourth type, the only white flower of the four, was the double recessive, which alone allowed the colour white to be manifested.

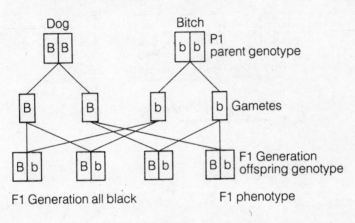

Black spotted Dalmatian dog (BB) ⎫ parent phenotype
Liver spotted Dalmatian bitch (bb) ⎭

Figure 3

THE MATING OF TWO HOMOZYGOUS DOGS

This is an excellent illustration of the difference between phenotype (appearance) and genotype (heredity). There are two phenotypes in the F.2 generation, red and white. But three genotypes exist, namely one double dominant red which is pure-breeding, two hybrid reds, and one pure-breeding double recessive white. These occur in the ratio 1:2:1 and genetically they are one homozygous red, one homozygous white and two heterozygous reds. The 1:2:1 ratio is only found when very large numbers are considered, and it cannot be expected to be accurate with small numbers. Just as a penny could be tossed ten times and come down heads (or tails) every time. If it were tossed 10,000 times the average would be about equal heads and tails. Averages of any kind are only valid in dealing with large numbers.

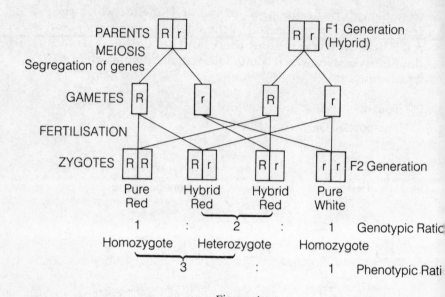

Figure 4

THE MATING OF TWO F1 HYBRIDS

It follows that any individual which displays a character known to be due to a recessive gene must inherit this gene from both parents, and therefore possess it in double dose and be pure-breeding. It must pass on the recessive gene to every one of its progeny, since it does not itself possess the opposite dominant gene. Recessive characters always breed true. An individual displaying a character known to be due to a dominant gene may possess it either in single dose when it will be hybrid for this character, or in double dose when it will be pure-breeding.

It will be evident in Mendel's experiments that the genes for red and those for white retain their identity, and though, because of dominance, white are masked by red in F.1, they sort themselves out in F.2.

Mendel's original work was done on peas and their colour but the principles of genetics which he discovered and which are expressed as Mendel's Laws are the same irrespective of whether one is dealing with the colour of pea plants or that of dogs. Let us take an example of black spotted Dalmatians and liver spotted (Fig. 3). Like the red and white peas, black spotted BB are dominant to liver spotted. Thus crossing a black spotted dog with a liver spotted bitch will result in all black offspring but these will not be homozygous but will be hybrids (Bb) or heterozygous. Mating these offspring, F.1 generation, will have the same effect as the mating of the two F.1 pea hybrids (Fig. 4). There would be three black spotted to one liver spotted F.2 generation and of the black spotted, one (BB) would be homozygous and breed pure and two (Bb) would be heterozygous, and being hybrids not breed pure (Fig. 5).

This basic breeding pattern led to Mendel's first Law, the *Law of Segregation* which basically states that genes normally present in pairs separate in the formation of the germ cells. The pairs are restored at fertilisation.

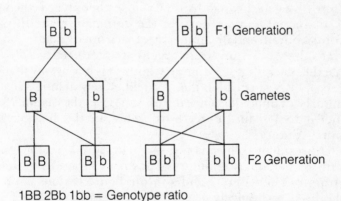

Figure 5

MATING BLACK SPOTTED HYBRID DALMATIANS (Bb)

The simple dominant-recessive relationship is by no means universal, it is, in fact, comparatively rare, but an understanding of it is the first step in genetics. It simplifies much which follows, and is probably the genetic process most useful to dog breeders, for it is concerned with coat colour and other characters. Moreover the double recessive gene pair is the cause of many hereditary faults. These can be identified and eliminated by using the genetic knowledge which is available on the subject.

Back-Cross

The back-cross is frequently used in dog breeding to identify a recessive gene, particularly those responsible for hereditary abnormalities. Animals homozygous for a particular pair of genes always breed true, the black spotted Dalmatian BB will always have black spotted offspring. However, the hybrid heterozygous black spotted dog Bb will produce some liver spotted offspring if mated to another animal homozygous to the (b) gene, in other words, if mated to a liver spotted animal. This is 'back-crossing to the recessive' and it is used to identify a recessive gene in an individual whose phenotype is the same as an animal homozygous for the dominant gene. In other words both BB and Bb animals are black but by mating Bb to a liver animal bb, if any liver progeny are produced it is obvious that the black dog is not homozygous. It is in this way that carriers of PRA can be identified by deliberately mating a suspect animal to a blind dog since the blindness, in the case of PRA is known to be due to recessive genes in the homozygous (pure) condition.

The result of such a mating is seen in Fig. 6 as applied to the form of hereditary blindness known as Progressive Retinal Atrophy. The letters S and s in the figure denote sight and blindness respectively.

It produces offspring half of which are heterozygous with normal vision and half homozygous and blind. The absence of any blind pups is presumptive evidence that the F1 sighted parent is pure breeding with two genes for sight. In such a case the result of the mating will repeat the result of the original P1 mating between two homozygotes, the one possessing two dominant genes for sight the other with two recessive genes for blindness.

Remembering that faults are in the main due to recessive genes, the importance of the back-cross to the parent, or of course to any other animal in the breed which displays the

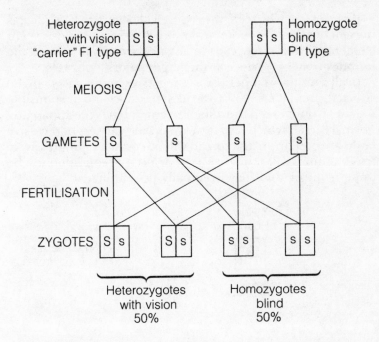

Figure 6

BACK-CROSS TO IDENTIFY PRA CARRIER

fault, is clear. The breeder will be aware that any animal showing the defect must inherit the gene for it in duplicate, and therefore from both parents, even if they have normal vision. They must be 'carriers' of the fault.

He will also be aware that the carrier of a single gene will pass it on to half its progeny and he will know how to identify the carrier by the process of test mating.

A positive result from test mating is conclusive and the appearance of even a single blind puppy indicates that the apparently normal parent undergoing the test is in fact a carrier and possesses a single gene for it.

Negative results are never as convincing as those which are positive. A radiographic picture, for instance, will show a suspected stomach ulcer in the majority of cases, the result will be positive.

If no ulcer can be seen, the report will be, not that no ulcer is present but that the photograph shows no sign of one. A slight element of doubt may exist in any negative result though the findings may be correct in the large majority of cases.

In all conditions inherited in a recessive manner it is not the afflicted animal which is the danger since no responsible breeder would breed from such an animal. It is the apparently normal carrier which is to be feared. If no carriers of recessive faults are bred from, the spread will be curtailed, progressively fewer animals will suffer from the defect, the condition will be under control, and may eventually be eliminated.

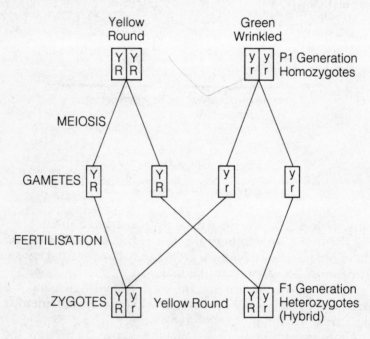

Figure 7

THE MATING OF DOUBLE DISSIMILAR HOMOZYGOTES

The incidence of diseases due to recessive genes depends, not only on those who suffer from them, but even more on the number of carriers, as they are called, which possess the gene in single dose but do not of course show evidence of the condition. With complete dominance, and we shall see later that dominance is not always complete, there is no means of recognizing a carrier of a recessive gene except by such a breeding test. If the condition is common in the breed concerned, or, in the case of humans, in the general population, research into pedigrees may give a clue. If the disease due to a recessive gene is rare, carriers will be very few, and generations may elapse before chance brings two carriers together in mating, when the condition will reappear to the mystification of breeders who know nothing of genetics.

Hereditary deafness, believed also to be due to a recessive gene pair, is not uncommon in some breeds of dogs, and it certainly behaves in the same way in most cases.

We have spoken of a positive breeding test in the identification of a recessive fault. One can say with certainty that any dog or bitch which is the parent of a blind puppy with the type of blindness we have been considering, is a carrier of the gene for this type of blindness. Both parents must have carried the gene for the condition to appear in the progeny, it is not the defect of one parent alone, it is the defect of both.

Mendel's Second Law, the Law of Independent Assortment in the Individual

This law states that when two or more pairs of genes are concerned, each pair segregates independently of every other pair. Later work in genetics has shown that there are exceptions to this rule if the genes are particularly closely related on the chromosome but broadly speaking it holds true. This law is of obvious value to breeders for it allows good points possessed by different individuals to be brought together in the same animal by selective matings. The law was formulated as a result of further work by Mendel with his peas but rather than discuss round and wrinkled, yellow and green peas it is probably more appropriate to discuss animal colours. Black for example (B), is dominant. Liver, as we have seen is recessive, (b), the hybrid (Bb) is always black. Black is a dense colour but there is a mutant allele which dilutes the colour so that a blue/grey is produced. The normal dense colour can be designated (D) and the dilute colour (d). According to Mendel's Second Law of Segregation, the colour genes B and b and the density of that colour D or d segregate independently thus the inheritance of d is identical to that of b, but since the genes are separate various combinations are possible as illustrated.

	BbDd ♂			BbDd ♀	F1 Heterozygote Meiosis segregation of genes

Gametes	BD	Bd	bD	bd	Gametes
BD	BBDD Black	BBDd Black	BbDD Black	BbDd Black	
Bd	BBDd Black	BBdd Blue	BbDd Black	Bbdd Blue	
bD	BbDD Black	BbDd Black	bbDD Chocolate	bbDd Chocolate	
bd	BbDd Black	Bbdd Blue	bbDd Chocolate	bbdd Lilac	

Figure 8

THE MATING OF DOUBLE HETEROZYGOTE HYBRIDS

Black is a dense colour hence the genotype BBDD, chocolate is also a dense colour so the genotype bbDD, blue is a dilute colour with a genotype BBdd. Chocolate dilute bbdd is totally recessive and is the lilac/grey colour found in the Weimeraner. Mendel found with his peas, and we will find with our breeding that these types did not occur in equal numbers but there is a definite ratio which works out at 9:3:3:1 when two heterozygous blacks BbDd are mated.

The diagram shows that, in the sixteen ways in which the gametes can combine, there will be nine different genotypes, but, because of dominance, only four different phenotypes.

This is another indication, were one needed, that appearance is no guide to breeding worth in respect of any individual character. Of the nine genetic patterns possible in this case, only two individuals, those at top left and bottom right diagonal corners, are pure-breeding for the respective dominant and recessive double characters.

It will be obvious that the presence of dominance dictates phenotype. When it is complete, the heterozygous individual resembles the dominant in appearance. In the absence of dominance heterozygous individuals differ in appearance from the homozygous, and we should therefore have more different phenotypes. This fact, however, does not in any way affect the manner of segregation.

Linkage

With the discovery of chromosomes and their behaviour at meiosis, it was seen that Mendel's Second Law could apply only when the pairs of allelic genes concerned were carried on different chromosomes. Two or more pairs, carried on the same chromosome, would tend to assort together. This is known as Linkage.

The dog has thirty-nine pairs of chromosomes. Each must carry a certain proportion of the large numbers of genes possessed by each animal. During meiosis each chromosome splits longitudinally, and each resulting half, known as a chromatid, moves as a unit. Genes which are carried on the same chromosome may, therefore, be expected to move as a block, remaining in their original combination and assorting together.

This is found to be the case, though cytology shows that linkage is not invariable and never complete.

Linkage may then be defined as the tendency of two or more pairs of allelic genes to assort together because they are carried on the same chromosome, instead of assorting independently in accordance with Mendel's Second Law. In this way genes carried on one chromosome will tend to be inherited together in what is known as 'linked inheritance'.

These instances where the Law of Independent Assortment ceased to apply were discovered early in the history of genetics, first by Bateson and Punnett, working together on sweet peas, and later by Morgan experimenting with Drosophila, the fruit fly.

Briefly they noted that certain genes, instead of assorting as expected, remained in their original parental formations. This discovery, and its subsequent explanation by linkage, marked an important milestone in the perfecting of the chromosome theory of heredity. We must think of linkage, not as merely a chance exception to Mendel's Second Law, but as something subject to its own laws.

It is obvious that if linkage were absolute and invariable, the chromosome would be the unit of inheritance rather than the gene. An animal would inherit chromosomes which all existed as such, in either sire or dam. And, tracing the pedigree further back, each would have existed as such in one or other of its grandparents. This is not the case, heredity suffers from no such restrictions. We shall see that the phenomenon of 'Crossing-over' explains why.

Crossing-over

We have seen that, during the complicated process of meiosis prior to the formation of the gametes, chromosome pairs split longitudinally into halves called chromatids. There is a tendency for homologous chromatids to come into close contact with each other, or become intertwined, during which part of one member of a pair may change places with part of its fellow member, resulting in a change of substance between them with the corresponding change or recombination of genes. Thus genes which were neighbours before this event, are neighbours no longer, and linkage is interfered with.

The diagram gives an idea of crossing-over in a greatly simplified form.

The process is complicated and hardly concerns us here, except to say that in the absence of crossing-over, or some equivalent method of 'shuffling and dealing' the hereditary units we call genes, variation, and with it evolution, could hardly have occurred.

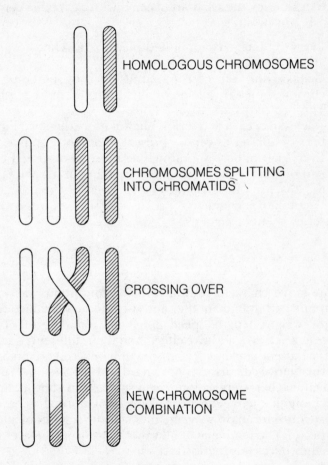

HOMOLOGOUS CHROMOSOMES

CHROMOSOMES SPLITTING INTO CHROMATIDS

CROSSING OVER

NEW CHROMOSOME COMBINATION

Figure 9

CROSSING-OVER

Organisms ill adapted to their environment would eventually have perished, and whole species would have been lost because no form suitably adapted to its environment was in existence. In fact this must have happened to the monstrous animals and reptiles of prehistory, which were probably so highly specialized that no suitabe form had been evolved which could adapt itself to a changing environment.

In considering the relations of genes with each other certain facts should be stressed:

1. Every gene has its appointed place on its chromosome, and this is known as its locus.
2. Genes lying on corresponding loci of homologous chromosomes are alleles, or allelomorphs, of each other. The two terms are synonymous.
3. Alleles may exist in a series, but not more than two members of any series can be present in any one animal.
4. Every pair of corresponding loci must be occupied by a pair of allelic genes, even if one member of the pair is for the absence of the character expressed by the other.
5. Quantitative characters are usually the expression of series of multiple alleles.

Quantitative Characters

Quantitative characters are a form of continuous variation from one extreme to another and include such characters as height, weight, length, speed, intelligence and so on. They arrive as a series of additive effects and their differences are of degree rather than kind. The distinction between quantitative and qualitative characters is not a hard and fast one since some qualitative characters, colour for instance, can show definite gradation in their gene expression. If a normal gene can mutate once it can do so again and again so a series of alleles can occur. The tendency of all inheritance is to the average, extremes become progressively rare.

It would seem that many characters of the dog will fall into this category; height, weight, length of limb bones, temperament, intelligence, teachability and so on, come to the mind at once.

Certain other aspects of conformation which the breeder knows from experience are strongly heritable, such as upright shoulders, straight stifles, shallow briskets and so on, would seem likely to be included in this category, if, as one may suppose, such complex characters are the expression of series of genes.

It is an interesting thought to consider whether these are linked series. Judging from the results of breeding from dogs possessing these and comparable faults of conformation, and the extreme frequency with which they are inherited, such a supposition seems tenable.

So far in this chapter we have studied the action of a single gene pair only, or of a single gene pair concerned with a second single gene pair in the mechanics of inheritance, neither pair having any genetic relationship with the other.

We have considered the relationship of a dominant gene with its recessive partner (its allele) in Mendel's original experiment with peas.

Dominance is probably the only genetic term in general use among dog breeders, and it is clear that many who use it do not understand its meaning, which is a precise one. Genes, or the characters expressed by them, may be dominant, that is, one member of a pair of allelic genes has the power of suppressing or masking that of the other member of the pair.

Dominance may be complete, but is not necessarily so. It can occur in all degrees from completeness to total absence. But the dominant recessive relationship is much less common than is generally supposed, and comparatively few characters are due to such a simple gene action. Those characters expressed by recessive genes [which must, it should be remembered, be inherited in duplicate for their effects to be produced], are more often harmful than useful.

We have seen the effect of dominance and have defined a dominant gene, and have mentioned that dominance may not always be complete. Incompleteness results in intermediate forms in varying degrees.

When dominance is incomplete or absent, a different phenotype occurs, for the hybrid resembles neither parent, but is somewhere intermediate between the two, whereas, as readers will remember, in true dominance the hybrid resembles its dominant parent.

Consider the merle dog, normal pigmentation (mm) will be sable and white, the homozygote mutant MM is nearly all white, has blue eyes and is usually deaf and for this reason is not usually kept. The heterozygote Mm, which in the case of complete dominance would resemble MM, e.g. white, is the merle collie which has white markings on the head and shoulders and a dapple coat of normal and so-called dilute, a bluish fawn pigmentation.

Other facts about gene relationships are important.

1. Different genes may have similar or identical effects, and by 'different' is meant a gene at a different locus from another. This means that a certain character may be caused in one case by one particular gene, and in another by a gene at a different locus.

2. Different genes may give rise to characters similar in nature but differing in degree. This is seen typically in the genetics of quantitative characters already considered.

3. Modifying genes, which act only on the expression of other genes. They have no known effect of their own, and can only be detected in the presence of other genes by their modifying effect.

4. Single genes may be responsible for multiple effects, probably a very widely spread phenomenon.

5. Genes belonging to different pairs, inherited independently, may act together to produce a particular character.

6. Lethal genes when homozygous cause the death of the individual. The dog does not have a well-known case of such a gene causing death before birth although the cat does. This is the Manx or tailless breed. All Manx cats are heterozygous, Mm, the homozygous MM dying in utero. The Manx can never be obtained as a true breeding animal. A common type of lethal gene produces a deformed pup at birth; this is a congenital lethal but not all congenital abnormalities are genetic. Some lethal genes do not cause immediate death but this can occur after an interval of weeks, months or even years. Many of the hereditary nervous conditions, e.g. progressive axonopathy in the Boxer fall into this category.

Epistasis. This is a form of gene action which has some of the features of dominance. The relationship has been aptly described as follows: 'When a certain gene is able to produce its full effect even in the presence of rival genes, it is said to be dominant if the rival gene is its allele and epistatic, if the rival gene is not its allele.'[1] While therefore a dominant gene is able to mask the effect of its partner on the corresponding locus, an epistatic gene can mask the effect of a gene which is not its partner, and which occurs on a different locus. Just as a dominant gene acts on its allele, so an epistatic gene acts on another gene which, though not its allele, is hypostatic to it. Coat colour gives examples of this.

Reversion. This may occur when crosses between true breeding varieties produce progeny which resemble some remote ancestor more than either parent. It is due to the reappearance of some old character owing to the reunion of two genes needed for its production, which, in the history of the animals' pedigrees, had become separated. This is more or less like the union of two heterozygote recessives, each carrying a single gene for some rare character.

Sex Linkage. The sex chromosomes contain many more genes than those concerned with sex. Such genes are associated with those for reproduction. Owing to this they are inherited together, and are carried on the X chromosome. Hence they are called sex-linked genes.

The X chromosome, to recapitulate, though present in duplicate in females, and only singly in males, is not concerned especially with femaleness, for it passes constantly back and forth between the sexes. The Y chromosome is possessed by males only, giving a genetic pattern for the sex chromosomes of XX female and XY male.

Sex linkage occurs whenever a mutation occurs in the X chromosome. A classical example involves tortoiseshell cats, the colour only occurs in the female and is determined by a mutant gene on the X chromosome. Dogs fortunately do not possess any coat colour sex linked genes but do have

---

[1]*The Genetics of the Dog.* Marca Burns. Commonwealth Agricultural Bureau. 1952.

haemophilia A, a fairly rare blood clotting disorder. Haemophiliac males are born to normal parents. The diagram sums up the situation.

Germ cells from dog
($X^H Y$)

	X^H	Y
X^H	$X^H X^H$ Normal	$X^H Y$ Normal
X^h	$X^H X^h$ Normal	$X^h Y$ Haemophiliac

Germ cells from female carrier ($X^H X^h$)

Figure 10

INHERITANCE OF HAEMOPHILIA IN THE DOG

Sex linkage is common in other species. In poultry, for instance, crossing a 'gold' breed, such as Rhode Island Reds, with a 'silver' breed, such as White Wyandottes, results in hybrid chicks the sex of which is at once obvious. The male chicks resemble the hen in colouring and the females resemble the cock.

11

How Genes Express Themselves

This chapter attempts to deal with the expression of genes in observable characters, in fact with the practical as counterpart of the theoretical.

How do genes bring about their effects in the organisms? How can colour, conformation, defects of physique or temperament, resistance or susceptibility to disease, or any other characteristic, be expressed in gene action?

Genes are parts of the body, they express themselves through the body processes we call physiology, they pass on the total inheritance from one generation to the next, and within the compass of two ultra-microscopic half cells, one inherited from each parent, lies the history of the species and the future of the resulting individual.

Genes act by chemical means to produce their effects. Both structure and function are the result of gene action, and the gene is the first cause of observable characters.

But genes are not the characters themselves and a long series of changes lie between the gene and its effect; let us say between a dark eye and the pigment laid down in the iris, if it is present in the heredity of the individual in question.

All heredity is subject to the influences of environment, good or bad, and the ultimate result of gene action depends on the balance between these two great forces.

The genetics of today is concerned largely with the problem of life itself, and involves the chemistry of chromosomes and genes, and especially of the sex chromosomes which alone take part in reproduction.

Enzymes. These are substances which are fundamental to body chemistry and which can produce chemical changes in other substances without themselves undergoing any chemical change.

For instance, starch is converted into a sugar through the action of the enzyme amylase in digestion; pepsin, with a number of other enzymes, converts the protein of food into its final components, the amino acids which are basic to life. The enzyme uricase, found in the liver, breaks down the uric acid in urine to its final stage of allantoin.

Exceptions to this reaction are found in man, the anthropoid apes, and curiously enough, the Dalmatian dog, none of which convert most of their uric acid into allantoin but excrete it as the acid.

The majority of dogs excrete small quantities of uric acid in their urine. The Dalmatian excretes large quantities. This is due to a recessive gene UA for high excretion which appears to be totally independent of the genes governing coat colouring. It is suggested that the UA gene was probably fixed in the breed by chance variation (Trimble & Keeler, 1938, Inheritance of High Uric Acid Excretion in Dogs, Journal Hered. *19* 280–289).

Hormones and Sexual Reproduction

We have already seen in considering the cell, that genes take part in sex determination in the embryo. They continue to exert an effect on sex development, either towards the male, through hormones called androgens secreted by the male testicle, or towards the female, through ovarian hormones called oestrogens.

The resulting sexual development of the individual and the fulfilment of its vital reproductive function depend on a complicated system of hormone actions. This system can be thought of as the intermediary between gene and the final result, the birth of living offspring.

Hormones are called the chemical messengers of the body; they do not act in isolation, but as members of a closely integrated team. They are the secretions of certain glands, known as endocrine glands, or ductless glands.

Some of these glands have a double function. In addition to an internal secretion which passes direct into the blood stream and is carried round in the circulation to affect any part of the body, they have an external secretion which passes direct by a tube or duct into a neighbouring structure, where its influence is direct and local.

The female ovary and the male testis are examples of organs with a double set of secretions, each being formed by a different part of the gland concerned.

The ovary secretes several hormones, some concerned with the development of female sex characters, others with the reproductive cycle, ovulation, conception, pregnancy, birth, lactation. The ovary's external secretion is its eggs. The main internal secretions of the testis are called androgens, which are responsible for male characters, its external secretion is its sperms.

The Reproductive Hormones

Apart from the female hormones, there are others also concerned in reproduction, and the most important are those of the *Pituitary Gland*, which has two lobes, anterior and posterior, situated in a tiny bony cavity at the base of the brain, the pituitary fossa.

The anterior pituitary gland has secretions controlling normal growth and development and also two main hormones concerned with reproduction. The first of these is called a *Follicle Stimulating Hormone*. This stimulates the formation and growth in the ovary of the structures which house the egg cells, the Graafian follicles. These follicles in turn produce *oestrogen*, which inhibits the first, follicle-stimulating hormone, and causes instead another hormone to be produced from the anterior pituitary, the *Luteinising Hormone*, which, with oestrogen, causes the lining of the uterus to be prepared for the eggs, the eggs to be ripened and shed from their follicles (Ovulation), and a body called the *Corpus Luteum* to be formed in the ovary. This body then produces another ovarian hormone called *Progesterone*, the next hormone in the sequence. This checks the activity of oestrogen, and also of the posterior pituitary gland secretion, known to everyone as pituitrin, which causes uterine contractions, and thus the uterus is kept in a state of quiescence during pregnancy and the embryo is enabled to develop without disturbance until full term is reached.

Finally, at this point, the influence of the ovarian hormones declines, notably that of progesterone allowing the posterior pituitary to come into action, causing the uterus to contract and the young to be born.

Luteinising hormone has another part to play, in most species. In association with oestrogen, it controls the development of the mammary gland.

The following simple diagram will illustrate this process, which is an excellent example of the closest hormone integration. It is obvious that a breakdown at any point in this series of reactions will affect the orderly course of pregnancy and parturition.

Genes also express themselves in the anatomy of the body, by means of hormones. The subject is too extensive to be considered here in any detail. A brief description, however, of the anatomy of the reproductive system may be of use as well as interest to the practical breeder.

The Anatomy of Reproduction

We have seen how the reproductive cells are set apart from the beginning for this special purpose, and how they are present in the gonads (the sex organs), and divide into gametes prior to fertilization. The gonads are the male testis and the female ovary, and the germ cells, or gametes, are sperms and ova.

The Dog

The essential sex organ in the dog is the testicle.

The *Testicle* is a paired organ, occupying the bag of skin, muscle and other tissue known as the scrotum, which has two compartments and hangs from the under wall of the belly. The testicles descend from the abdominal cavity where they are developed during intra-uterine life, to occupy the scrotum at birth or soon after. Though immature at this early age they can be recognized as two slight swellings in the two halves of the scrotum. The testicles, one or both, may fail to descend

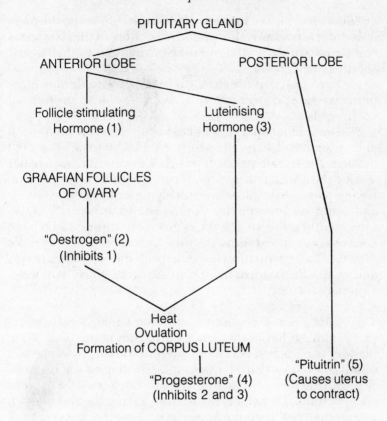

PITUITARY GLAND

ANTERIOR LOBE   POSTERIOR LOBE

Follicle stimulating   Luteinising
Hormone (1)   Hormone (3)

GRAAFIAN FOLLICLES
OF OVARY

"Oestrogen" (2)
(Inhibits 1)

Heat
Ovulation
Formation of CORPUS LUTEUM

"Progesterone" (4)   "Pituitrin" (5)
(Inhibits 2 and 3)   (Causes uterus
                            to contract)

Figure 11

REPRODUCTIVE HORMONES

normally, descent may be delayed or absent. The condition in which one testicle has failed to descend is known popularly as monorchidism, that in which both testicles are absent from the scrotum, cryptorchidism. A more accurate way of naming these conditions would be to use the word *Cryptorchid* for any dog which had either or both of its testicles absent from the scrotum, and preface it with unilateral when one testicle was absent, bilateral when both were missing. The true monorchid is a dog which possesses only one testicle, the other having failed to develop. If both testicles fail to develop the animal is known as anorchid.

The reason for the location of the testicles outside the body is one of temperature, the lower temperature of the scrotum as compared with the abdomen favouring the vitality of the sperm cells.

We have seen that the testicle is a gland with a double function. We are concerned now with the manufacture of sperm cells.

The individual sperm is microscopic. It has a small head and a long flail-like tail, which enables it to propel itself through the female passages to reach the uterine horn. After leaving the testicle, the sperms eventually arrive at the urethra, having passed first into a fine tube lying alongside the testicle and acting as a temporary storehouse. From the tail of this tube, another, the *vas deferens*, is given off, through which the sperms reach the urethra, the tube by which urine leaves the bladder. These structures, together with blood vessels, nerves and lymph ducts, form the spermatic cord, which, as it were, suspends the testicle.

The *Prostate Gland* is another important male organ of reproduction. It lies in the pelvis, surrounding the neck of the bladder and the first part of the urethra, varying from the size of a hazel nut to that of a walnut, according to the breed of dog. During the act of mating, the prostate secretes a copious alkaline fluid. This enters the urethra, taking the sperms with it, and the combined fluids proceed along this passage until they are expelled in copulation.

The *Penis* is long and pointed, the point being protectd by a sheath which is retracted during mating. It contains a bone, and consists of muscle, nerves and lymph ducts, together with many loose spaces, which become engorged during sexual excitement, causing the penis to swell and become rigid. This swelling is especially marked at the base, and constitutes an almost globular mass of tissue, which enables the dog to 'tie' during copulation, when it is tightly gripped by the circular band of muscle fibres at the opening of the bitch's vulva. The presence of this circular muscle has an important bearing on the tie, and if it is ineffective the chances of conception may be reduced.

The Bitch

The essential sex gland is the *Ovary*, which bears the egg cells, or ova. These do not ripen until sexual maturity is reached, marked by the first heat, and as we have seen, they are ripened by the action of two interdependent hormones, the luteinising hormone and oestrogen. From this time to the end of her life, the bitch ripens a number of egg cells at each heat, though fertility is naturally impaired with advancing years.

The *Ovaries*, which are paired, are small flattened oval bodies each enclosed in a membraneous sac, lying on either side of the abdomen near the kidneys. When, as the result of hormone stimulation during heat, the egg cells ripen and are shed, the eggs burst through the covering of the ovary to make their way through a fringed funnel-shaped opening into the uterine or Fallopian tube, which is continuous with the uterine horn. In the uterine horns the eggs are fertilized by the ascending sperms, and there, attached to the walls, the fertilized eggs grow into individuals capable of leading an independent existence.

The *Uterus* consists of a small body and two horns, rising from each side of the upper part of the body. The body plays no part in harbouring the developing embryos, its lower portion ends in a neck or cervix as it is called, which leads through an opening, which is normally closed during pregnancy, to the vagina, and thence to the external part of the genital passage, the vulva. The passage of the whelp from its position in the uterine horn through the body of the uterus, through a dilated cervix into the vagina, and out at the vulva constitutes the event of birth.

The *Placenta* or afterbirth, is a flattened pancake-like organ, composed mainly of blood vessels, by which the developing embryo is attached to the wall of the uterine horn, and in which the exchange of maternal and foetal circulation takes place. By way of the umbilical cord, attached to foetus and placenta, the maternal blood supplies oxygen and nutrient materials to the foetus, and carries away the waste products in exchange. Cord and placenta are covered with membranes which are reflected to enclose the foetus. Placental hormones stimulate the flow of milk, and probably help the uterus to return to normal after whelping.

The *Mammary Glands*. The breasts of the bitch are arranged in two rows, extending from the armpit to the groin on either side of the midline of belly and thorax.

They are usually ten in number, five on either side, but eight are not uncommon. The hindmost breasts are usually best developed, being larger than those further forward, and secreting more milk. The nipples consist of tough fleshy tissue, perforated by a number of holes, the orifices of the milk ducts.

During the latter part of pregnancy, especially in a matron, the breasts enlarge, and the nipples become more prominent, though it is unusual for milk to be secreted until near whelping time, and, in the case of maiden bitches, until whelping is actually in progress. Many unmated, or even maiden bitches secrete milk in varying amounts at the time when puppies would have been born had mating taken place. The occurrence is normal, and need cause no anxiety, but should not be stimulated by rubbing, which tends to encourage it.

Heredity and Disease

Many developmental conditions and several diseases are known to be of genetic origin in dogs. Malformations can also be inherited. Inherited diseases, particularly those affecting the eye and the nervous system are a source of worry in many breeds. Bony conditions such as Hip Dysplasia and Ununited Anconeal Processes as well as Osteochondritis Dessicans may be multifactorial. Cryptorchidism whether unilateral or bilateral is determined in part by heredity although this is hotly contested in some quarters. It is also sex limited in that females are not able to exhibit the defect but they could carry it and pass the liability to their sons. The bilateral cryptorchid is sterile.

Immunity is resistance to disease, and is used especially in infectious disease. It can exist in two forms, Natural and Acquired. We know little of the mechanism of inheritance of *Natural Immunity*, but at least two facts are recognized.

1. It has a hereditary basis.

2. It is specific, that is, specialized for each infection, and not general for all. An individual may be immune to the effects of one virus and highly susceptible to those of another. There is believed to be some sort of breed immunity in dogs to certain infections, and increased susceptibility to others.

Acquired Immunity is brought about by an attack of the disease in question, either natural, as the result of chance infection, or planned, by inoculation, either with an attenuated form of the infecting organism or by its toxins. This is known as *Active Immunity*, a sub-division of the acquired type. The production of active immunity is brought about by stimulation of the body's protective reactions in the face of infection, to produce substances called antibodies. These attack the invaders, and if numerous and powerful enough, recovery takes place. Antibodies remain in the blood for varying periods, according to the disease concerned, and as long as they are present, they protect from another attack of the same disease. This immunity is sometimes life-long. The presence of antibodies can be detected, and their strength determined, by certain blood tests. *Passive Immunity* is produced by the administration, usually by injection, of blood serum containing a large amount of antibodies, the result of a successfully resisted infection by the animal which supplied it.

The duration of passive immunity is usually shorter than that of any form of active immunity. It is useful in giving protection when it is known that infection may be encountered or immediately after it has occurred.

There may be cases in which the protective mechanism fails to respond, or in which the attack is so virulent that defences are overwhelmed before they have time to come into action; in such cases the outlook is gloomy. Modern drugs, and especially antibiotics, are of great value in treatment. Moreover, multiple vaccines are now combined in a single dose, to give protection against several different infections with one inoculation. Refusal to make use of the protection we have against the infections of today, and very good protection it is, would appear to lack any reasonable basis. So-called 'Natural Remedies' are often advocated; the term has no precise meaning.

All remedies are derived from natural sources of one kind or another, and certainly nothing could be more natural than the protective substances manufactured by the body itself. Neither is the attempt to isolate the dog completely from every possible source of infection to be recommended, to keep an animal as it were as nearly as possible in a glass case. Such methods invariably break down. To deprive a dog of any opportunity of acquiring active immunity of any kind may be to deprive it of the chance of survival in any serious infection.

The best protection we can give our dogs is first to refuse to breed from weaklings, second to give them a good environment with all that this entails, and third to have them inoculated against the killing diseases of dogs at the proper time.

The Genetics of Coat Colour

The genetics of coat colour in the different breeds of dogs is complex compared with, for example, cats. However much work has been recently carried out in this field and the interested reader is referred to *Genetics for Dog Breeders* by Roy Robinson, FIBiol, Pergamon Press 1982.

12

Breeding and Breeding Systems

The gap between practical breeding and the genetic theory we have been considering is obvious. Is any advantage to be gained by 'bothering' with all this theory? Shall we do any better than we have done in the past by using the old methods of trial and error? How can we identify genes, and, if we can, can it be possible for more than a very few characters? How can we relate characters to genes and genes to characters? Are there perhaps any drawbacks to the use of genetic principles in breeding? Would it not, in any case, be simpler to make use of what genetic knowledge has made available without troubling to grasp the underlying principles?

Anyone who has persevered thus far with this book will probably have made up his mind that even if genetics is no royal road to success and provides no infallible recipe for breeding champions, it is still useful and interesting, and that an intelligent interest in and understanding of the principles on which it is based, can raise the status of the dog breeder to that of the craftsman, who knows what he is doing and the tools he is working with.

Let us consider some of the advantages of breeding on genetic lines.

1. Genetics has opened the door to the quickest method of eliminating faults due to the action of single gene pairs in the dominant-recessive relationship. Many faults are due to recessive genes.
2. Genetics has shown how desirable characters can be introduced into strains which lack them.
3. Genetics provides a reasonable basis for and explanation of the various systems of breeding which before were founded more or less on rule of thumb.

4. It enables breeding to be planned, and not a haphazard affair such as the all-too-common method of choosing a sire on appearance alone, without thought of ancestors or progeny.

The breeder's tools are the same today as in the past; selection, crossing and in-breeding have not altered. But a knowledge of heredity enables them to be used more skilfully and purposefully, and it shortens the time needed to produce results.

The dog breeder's task is far different from that of other livestock breeders; he wants an overall high standard, not exaggerated in any direction, whereas breeders of cattle, for instance, breed for single, or at most double characters, milk or beef production, or a combination of the two in a dual-purpose animal. The race-horse breeder requires speed or stamina, and, providing his horse has one or the other, he does not worry overmuch about appearance. It is perhaps significant that appearance and performance do often go together.

The dog breeder must decide at the outset of his breeding career just what his main aim is to be. If his only desire is to breed the occasional good dog which will excel in the show-ring, and he cares little about the general quality of his stock, one form of breeding is probably as good as another. He will select the mates for his bitches on appearance alone, and chance will dictate the outcome, which may easily produce a good result from his point of view, if he obtains one or two outstanding puppies in a mediocre litter. But disappointment comes when, in turn, his outstanding animals are bred from; except by a lucky chance they are unlikely to reproduce their own excellence, for many of their genes will be in the herozygous state and the animals will not breed true for many of their characters.

If our breeder's aim is, on the other hand, to improve the generaly quality of his stock so that his dogs gain steadily in type, conformation, temperament and the rest, he will learn some of the lessons of heredity, and adopt breeding methods which will ensure that his stock breeds more and more true in various important directions, his all-round standard will be high, and the outstanding animal will still appear from time to time because his stock being in the main homozygous in good qualities, will pass on the genes for these qualities to all their progeny. The breeder will know fairly accurately what to expect in all his litters. He will know what faults he need not fear and what others he must guard against, he will know the good points he wishes to introduce and how to set about it.

Genetics has already taken charge of plant breeding, and breeders of farm stock have lost no time in availing themselves of its help. Dog breeders lag behind in this respect. Their work is still more art than science and may always remain so, for the 'eye for a dog' is inborn and not to be acquired from books. But there is no reason why art should not be combined with science, the 'green fingers' with the knowledge now available, there need be no antagonism between the two.

Has the pursuit of genetic knowledge and the application of its principles any drawback? In theory certainly, though hardly in practice. The aim of the dog breeder is to produce stock in which all the genes responsible for 'desirable' characters are in the homozygous state, they breed true because their gene pairs for any given character are alike. It should be mentioned that 'desirable' from the show-ring point of view may not always be desirable in the interests of the breed concerned.

Now, in so far as homozygosity applies to a few desirable characters it is a good aim. It will be realized, however, that even if it were possible, it would be highly undesirable for animals to be homozygous for all their characters, bad as well as good. Such a condition would prevent any change in the hereditary pattern and put an entire stop to the variability which is an essential of evolution. Practically, of course, there is no possibility of any such thing.

If a study of genetics, however elementary, allows the breeder, as it does, to fix good characters, good temperament, good conformation, good constitution and good appearance, then it is useful. Good temperament should be essential to every breeder, good conformation will not only please the eye, but will ensure good action, and general balance, and, as applied to the many important organs which carry on the life functions of the animal, it will enable these to be performed well and safely.

If, in addition, the breeder is able, by means of genetics, to detect and get rid of hereditary faults and to introduce virtues which may be lacking, then its usefulness cannot be denied.

Apart from deliberately breeding in deformities which interfere with reproduction or any other of the vital functions, in response to show-ring fashions, the breeder is not likely to do any harm. In any case Nature has a way of taking a hand at times to redress the balance, though her methods are often cruel and wasteful.

We have shown how faults can be bred out by a system of back-crosses. Let us now see how a desired character can be introduced. And, for example, let us take erect ears, to be introduced into a drop-eared breed. Erect ears are considered by many authorities to be dominant to the drop variety, and for the present purpose we will assume that they are.

It can be done, though there would certainly be more difficulties on the way than the calculation shows. The process would be lengthy if the animals used were of two different breeds. It would have two aims.

1. The introduction of erect ears into a drop-eared breed.
2. The elimination of all other traces of the erect-eared breed used in the process.

A start would be made with two pure-breeding parents (P.1); the one dominant and homozygous for erect ears, EE, the other recessive and homozygous for drop ears, ee.

Step 1.   Mating of the parents, EE × ee gives a litter of heterozygotes, all therefore hybrids with the formula Ee, and therefore not true breeding. These are the F.1 generation.

Step 2.   Mating of all the F.1 members back to the recessive drop-eared parent, the typical back-cross already studied. The result is the usual 50% of each type, the typical back-cross ratio, Ee ee. Experience has shown that the resulting prick-eared hybrids (Ee) are likely to resemble the drop-eared breed in appearance to a considerable degree. The prick-eared members of the litter are still, of course, hybrids.

Step 3.   The same back-cross of the prick-eared members has to be continued, in each case back to the drop-eared dog, until all traces of the prick-eared dog have disappeared, except its prick ears. When this point has been reached, all the prick-eared animals in the litter resemble the drop-eared dog in every respect but ears.

Step 4. The most typical of the erect-eared specimens, still all hybrids for ear carriage, must then be mated together, and the result will be the F.2 generation with its ratio of 1 : 2 : 1., one dominant and homozygous with erect ears; two heterozygous, and, owing to dominance, erect eared; one recessive and homozygous with drop ears.

The average of pure-breeding erect-eared dogs is seen to be one in four only. And this will be our breeding animal for the next generation.

Step 5. But we have not yet identified our pure-breeding prick-eared dog from among the majority which display prick ears, two out of every three of which can be expected to be heterozygous.

The back-cross mating of the possible heterozygote to the homozygous recessive, the original drop-eared dog, or a similar one, test-mating in fact, is the necessary final step. If all the heterozygotes are test-mated, the occurrence of a single drop-eared puppy in any litter is evidence that the prick-eared parent is not pure-breeding, but a carrier of the recessive gene for drop ears.

The gene for the erect ear is introduced at the first cross, and its presence is indicated, owing to dominance, even if only in single dose. The possibly lengthy series of back-crosses to the original drop-eared animal (or breed) is the method of eliminating all traces of the second breed except its ears. Within a single breed the process would be shorter.

Figures are of course averages and are not likely to be accurate except in cases of very large numbers.

Only by breeding out recessive genes can they be got rid of finally. We have already seen how a recessive gene for some rare character can be passed on through generations, quite unsuspected from the appearance or behaviour of the animals concerned, until it comes to light by a mating with another animal carrying the duplicate gene, and this may be exceedingly rare if the character is uncommon. Heredity teaches us that such a character is persistent and the gene for it did not disappear, it merely lay dormant during an indefinite number of generations. In fact, it must have been present in the ancestry of both partners and have been handed on in single doses for perhaps many generations until chance brought two members of such a gene pair together. The usual argument is that a character cannot be hereditary because neither children nor grandchildren, nor great-grandchildren of an affected animal have shown the defect. It is clear how fallacious such an argument is.

The importation of a recessive character into a breed is much easier than its elimination, for one reason only. It is that any recessive character must be due to a double dose of the gene concerned. Going back to our dogs' ears which we have assumed to be dominant if erect, and recessive if dropped, the erect-eared dog *may* not breed true, the recessive drop-eared dog *must* breed true, it carries no genes for erect ears and therefore cannot pass any on to its progeny. The recurring difficulty with the heterozygote never occurs in dealing with the introduction of a recessive character because the character can only be displayed in the presence of two recessive genes.

In new breeds created by man, it is practically impossible to eliminate completely all the characters of the original ancestors. It is noticeable in Boxers, for example, one of whose original parents was a white English Bull bitch, that to this day near white, or even all white puppies occur in many litters, an illustration of the persistence of hereditary factors in spite of all attempts to eliminate them.

There is scope for even the smallest breeder to add to the knowledge of canine genetics, in which the heredity of so many characters remains to be worked out, and to learn himself something practical of the relationship of genes to the characters they express, by observing and writing down details of all his litters, starting with the parents, and giving full particulars of pedigree, with all colours mentioned when known. The numbers of puppies in each litter, coat, nose, eye-rim and eye colour, conformation, temperament, tail carriage. All noticeable features for each puppy should be included, and any faults of any kind would complete the picture. A great deal might be learnt from any concerted effort of this kind, and breeders would certainly find much useful information as well as great interest.

To be even a little genetically minded makes breeding more exciting and incidentally more successful. Each dog, each litter, is not then an event in isolation, but a link in a chain, receiving from previous links, handing on to future links, and the inheritance is to some extent in the hands of the breeder. He can observe, if he will, the sort of stock he is using, he can notice the characters, from what dogs they come, and to what dogs they are handed on; where this fault came from, which strain or animal excels in that virtue, tracing both virtues and faults backwards and forwards across the generations, trying to see as many related dogs as possible of those concerned, and remembering that the only true test of breeding worth is the progeny test.

Selection

Consciously or not the breeder is always using the method of selection which needs genetic variation on which to work. Without variation there can be no change in the genetic pattern, and characters arising from the genetic pattern are the only ones to be inherited. Selection does not produce new genes, it produces new phenotypes, by recombining existing genes. Thus selection differs from mutation. It enables breeders to bring together by suitable matings the animals believed to possess desirable genes or gene combinations, and eventually to fix these in the homozygous state, which ensures that the animal possessing them must pass them on to all its progeny. If selection is wise, the appearance and breeding worth of stock can improve with each generation.

It follows, therefore, that whether the breeder knows it or not, he is always dealing with genes though he is actually concerned with the characters the genes express. A breeder cannot often know that a given character, whether one he wishes to introduce or one he wishes to breed out, is governed by a single gene pair or a gene complex the behaviour of either of which he is able to foretell. If he has this knowledge, and it is available in connection with certain characters, mainly faults and defects, his position is strengthened.

Records help greatly, and the habit of mind which considers constantly the relationship between what is noticed in stock, and the possible genetic reasons for it, is likely to result in a good knowledge of the heredity of a breed which will stand the breeder in good stead in all his breeding operations.

Breeding Stock

The serious breeder will choose his breeding stock with the greatest care, knowing that initial mistakes may be costly. Parents should be chosen with a view to complementing each other, to improving each other's weak points and to strengthening and fixing good points. Selection should be not only on appearance, but on pedigree and progeny. Pedigrees are only of value if the breeder knows something of the animals concerned, their faults and their virtues. Progeny will show whether or not either faults or virtues are likely to be inherited. Names on a pedigree are no help without this knowledge. We have seen that it is risky to choose mates by phenotype alone, for, like an iceberg, the greater part of the dog's hereditary pattern may lie hidden beneath the surface. The most famous champions may be heterozygous for many of their show points, and undesirable genes may be concealed beneath an almost faultless exterior. It can never be repeated too often that the only true test of breeding-worth is the progeny test. A sire which can pass on his good points to a number of different bitches of different strains is likely to have many of them in the homozygous state, and will therefore pass them to all his progeny. This is what is meant by prepotency.

Prepotency, a word commonly in use among dog breeders with this precise meaning which has a definite significance, is the power of passing on good qualities, for the reason that they are possessed in duplicate and must therefore be inherited by all offspring. Prepotency for any point indicates therefore simple homozygosity in respect of that point. It is the most valuable attribute of the stud dog and also the bitch, though her opportunities for passing on her virtues are necessarily fewer.

In a carefully bred strain, bred to a system making use of genetic knowledge, a sensible breeder will fix many good points in the homozygous state, and his stock will be more likely to breed true than that of a chance-bred dog, even if almost every ancestor should be a champion. The wise breeder knows that to be a champion is a proof of individual excellence and not of genetic worth. This is not to decry champions as such. A champion who shows evidence of careful selective breeding in its pedigree and appearance is the ideal. A champion which crops up suddenly in a strain which has never bred any outstanding dogs is most unlikely to pass on his good points to his progeny. It is safe to say that it is fatal for any dog and bitch to possess a serious fault in common, however excellent they are in other respects. A fault on one side should not be corrected by the opposite fault on the other, but by as great a degree of perfection in the point as possible.

Should a dog with a serious fault ever be used in breeding? This must depend to some extent on the faults and on the genetic make-up of the other parent. Faults are likely to be passed on. If the other parent excels in the particular point the F.1 generation will probably not manifest the defect, but they, or some of them, will certainly carry a gene for it. The greatest care should therefore be taken when these animals in their turn are mated, to breed back to the original good point, and not to any animal even slightly failing in it, otherwise the fault is certain to appear in some members of the F.2 generation.

Should mediocrities be used in breeding programmes? These are dogs with no especially serious faults, but equally with no particular virtues. Bitches are often described as 'perhaps not show specimens but likely to make good brood bitches'. Complete mediocrity is as serious a breeding defect as a single serious fault, in fact more so, for a single fault can be got rid of; it is dependent on a single gene or at least a very few, whereas mediocrity denotes the absence of any positive virtues and such animals are more than likely to pass on their own mediocrity. The outstanding dog, with perhaps one serious fault, is a different proposition. If carefully bred he will possess many of his desirable genes in duplicate, with all that this implies. His serious fault can be eliminated without too much trouble, by genetic means, and even with the method of the average non-genetic breeder, using simple commonsense in his breeding methods, such a fault can be hidden for generations, though the gene for it may still exist in single state.

The writer would not hesitate to use such a dog, the one proviso being that after such a mating, the next generation should be bred back to the perfection in the point at issue. A first-class dog with an obvious fault is likely to be a much better breeding proposition than the mediocrity.

Requirements of Breeding Stock

The basic requirements of breeding stock are:

1. *Type*, the sum of the characteristics in their ideal form which distinguish one breed from another. Type is a matter in which every aspect of the dog is concerned, including temperament. Type may change as the years go by, perhaps almost insidiously, but once true type is lost the breed as such is lost. Every experienced breeder and competent judge recognizes the importance of type, perhaps the first essential of show stock. Other defects can be bred out or minimized; type is fundamental and indispensable.

2. *Correct Conformation*. In its widest sense this includes not only anatomy, but function, the bones, joints and muscles, and the organs which carry on the life processes. The animal body is not a mere haphazard assembling of parts, it is a highly organized confederation of interlocking members, each essential to the working of the whole. The skeleton, with its bones, joints and attached muscles, the team of internal organs, the blood which supplies food to the entire body, and the brain and nervous system which exercise overriding control over the whole – all these must function harmoniously and in closest co-operation, if the body is to remain healthy. Perhaps at this stage we might look back and marvel that the minute cell, the zygote, has, controlled and conditioned by its genes and its environment, grown to this little cosmos, the animal body.

3. *Correct Temperament.* Every breeder knows what a good temperament means, and how important it is to show dog or companion. Unfortunately it is often neglected in favour of show points, and the price of neglect is heavy. Nervousness, bad temper, unreliability, all these may be inherited, though they are sometimes the result of environment. Each breed too has its traditional temperament, characteristic of its breed, and a valuable part of breed type.

Dogs with nervous or savage temperaments should never be used in breeding, however great their physical perfections.

The reader will realize by now that, with all the care in the world, breeding results cannot be accurately and completely foretold. The breeder must do his best, in the light of the knowledge available, and can then only wait and see what Mendelian segregation and recombination has in store for him. He can be certain that breeding will never be a penny-in-the-slot affair, there will be plenty of surprises, pleasant and otherwise.

Before passing on to discuss breeding systems, a few words should be said about relationship.

Relationship has an exact genetic meaning. As between any two animals, it is the probability that, insofar as they have a common ancestry, they will be alike in a greater proportion of their genes than would any unrelated members of the species.

Relationship may be *direct*, from parent to child or *collateral*, in which both animals are descended in varying degree from a common ancestor, e.g. brothers, half-brothers, nieces, cousins, etc.

In any small population such as a breed, and especially in the numerically smaller breeds, and still more in a strain within a breed, there are likely to be many genes in common. Relationship denotes similarity above the average.

Strain. This term, which should denote relationship, is often used when no relationship exists. A strain is a family, the members of which are related to each other more or less closely. It is misused when applied to unrelated dogs, and the fact that they may have a prefix in common has no bearing on the issue.

Bloodlines. This is another term often used to denote similarity of heredity by virtue of relationship, that is to say that all members of any litter must have the same heredity because of their relationship. Now, as readers will have realized, this is not so. We have seen that genes segregate, some going into one fertilized egg and others into another, so that, even with the closest in-breeding, no two members of any litter are identical, unless they be uni-ovular twins, arising from one egg cell. These are believed to be rare in dogs. It is thus possible to find one member of a litter lacking every characteristic which made another member a good dog, as many a breeder has discovered.

In implying the inevitable inheritance of identical characters by reason of relationship, therefore, the term 'bloodlines' is misleading. It is a survival from the vague conception of blended inheritance. Every parent passes on to all its progeny only a half, and that a sample half, of its own inheritance, and the sample as we have seen, can be good, bad, or mixed.

The simplest and most fundamental relationship is that of parent and child. This is 50%. Half the genes of any animal are identical with half of each parent. The inheritance from grandparents need not be exactly 25% from each, owing to Mendelian segregation and recombination in the intervening generation. Every such segregation will probably halve the fraction of duplicate genes inherited.

A name, therefore, however famous, appearing once, say, in the fifth generation of a pedigree has very little influence, roughly 3%, and many ancestors of less merit, it must be remembered, may each contribute an equal amount to the total inheritance.

Turning to collateral relationship, full brothers and sisters (full sibs, as they are called) are also related 50%, half-brothers and half-sisters 25%.

All such proportions are averages, estimated from the laws of probability. If a high proportion of the genes of either parent should be homozygous, the chances are that any two of its offspring will possess more identical genes, and therefore be more alike than the expected average.

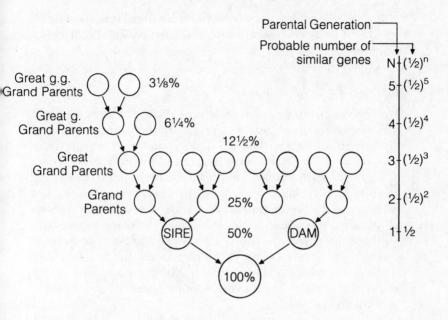

Figure 12
RELATIONSHIP
The fraction of genes likely to come to an individual from its direct ancestry

A. Random Matings.
B. Mating Like-to-Like.
 1. As Individuals.
 2. By pedigree.
  (*a*) In-breeding.
  (*b*) Line-breeding.
C. Mating Unlikes. (Deliberately mating unrelated animals.)

Random Matings

This is hardly a system, and is only included for the sake of completeness. It implies the mating of individuals neither more nor less alike than the average of the animals concerned.

Random mating is not controlled by man, it is sometimes restricted by Natural Selection, and propinquity must play a large part.

Like-to-Like as Individuals

By this system mates are chosen for their similarity in desirable points. It may be structure, decoration or any other. It is an attempt to fix a wished-for quality, and may be successful or not, according to the gene pattern of the individual. It is a specialized form of selection. Whilst in-breeding is the mating of individuals likely to possess the same genes, like-to-like matings is between individuals with the same or similar characters; it is phenotypic, but tends to assure some slight similarity of genotype above the average. In practice it works out as mating best to best either in general merit or in a high degree of some desirable character. Mediocre and bad are left out of the picture. Thus a very definite selection goes hand in hand with the method.

It is difficult or impossible to find animals alike in every desirable point, and so it often happens that mates are chosen for similarity in one or two outstanding characters. Such qualities, however, by no means always depend on simple allelic gene pairs, but more often on complicated gene complexes, and they are also influenced by environment. Thus, while in-breeding may be expected to bring together mates likely to possess many genes in common, this does not necessarily apply in breeding like to like. Nothing like fixation of type can be expected from this method. Widely used in a small group, it would tend to produce a population of extremes in respect of characters in which it was used. It would be no help if an intermediate type were desired.

This form of mating is therefore useful in securing desired phenotype, and so, for example, will often provide a good show specimen. But it can only be fixed for breeding purposes, by recourse to in-breeding. The like-to-like method has been widely used in the past and still is. It finds a place in dog breeding when a breeder possesses an animal which conforms so closely to the ideal as to present no fault he would wish to breed out, and he therefore chooses a mate as like it as possible in all respects. If the result is satisfactory he should remember its temporary nature, and fix it by means of in-breeding.

Like-to-like Breeding by Pedigree

In-breeding

In-breeding has been and still is a matter of controversy. In most cases it is not the method which is at fault, but its application to unsuitable stock by breeders with little knowledge of basic hereditary principles.

The aim of in-breeding is to duplicate good points, as the result of inheriting genes for these points from both parents, that is to say, to increase homozygosity for as many desired characters as possible. Chosen mates must be closely related, because these are more likely to possess genes in common. In-breeding must be carried on for several generations to give any useful results. The early stages may well be disappointing, but Mendelian segregation does allow characters to be sorted out within the second generation. Culling must be the invariable accompaniment of in-breeding, certainly in its early stages, and possibly for several generations.

The essence of in-breeding is relationship, which is usually the closest possible, parent-child, or brother-sister. The term is sometimes used to include less close relationships such as half-brother and half-sister, grandparent and grandchild, cousins and so on.

This method has many advantages and a number of disadvantages.

Advantages of In-breeding

1. It fixes type more quickly than any other method.
2. It tends to the formation of distinct families within a breed, and selection based on family is better than selection based on individuals.
3. It is valuable as a test of breeding worth, that is of genotype. Mating a dog to a number of his daughters is a severe test of breeding value. Hidden faults may be brought to light, which to the serious breeder can only be

an advantage, for it gives the opportunity to breed
them out.

4. It fixes favourable characters in the homozygous state,
and is, in fact, the only way of fixing them with any
certainty.

5. By increasing homozygosity within a strain therefore, it
increases the prepotency of individual animals.

Disadvantages of In-breeding

1. It affects all genes, and not merely the chosen few on the
action of which the breeder has concentrated. It therefore
fixes faults just as readily as virtues, and even more readily,
the harassed breeder may sometimes think. Injudicious
in-breeding is likely to lead quickly to deterioration of
stock.

2. It is therefore no method for the novice, for much
knowledge both of pedigrees and the actual dogs named
in them is needed, as well as their ancestors and their
progeny.

3. It may break up and disperse favourable gene combinations for desirable characters, which will then suffer
accordingly.

4. It needs outstanding animals, of which few may be
available.

5. It may easily perpetuate a line of mediocrities, a condition
more difficult to improve than the occurrence of even
quite serious isolated faults, because it is due to a general
lack of merit in practically all important characters.

6. Severe culling is necessary, and this is always sad for those
who love dogs.

In short, in-breeding is a powerful tool, it may be a
dangerous one.

Line-breeding

Much that has been said about in-breeding applies to line-
breeding, which may be defined as the mating of individuals
within a particular line of descent in the attempt to keep the
progeny as closely related as possible to a particular ancestor
of outstanding merit.

This method is popular among all breeders of pedigree stock.

Although, strictly speaking, it is a form of in-breeding, it seems to miss completely the odium which in some quarters is attached to that method. This is possibly because line-breeding is a less powerful breeding tool, capable neither of the spectacular success, nor of the dismal failure which occasionally occurs in close in-breeding.

The chief feature is relationship to a particular ancestor, and this animal should be recognized while he is still alive, and matings direct to him are possible. In this way his influence can be greatly extended. If, on the other hand, he appears only once on each side of a pedigree and all matings must be made to his descendants, his influence is greatly watered down. Relationship is the chief feature of this method, and just as much in-breeding must be practised as is needed to maintain relationship.

Excellence in the animal to which bitches are line-bred is also essential for success, line-breeding to mediocrity is not likely to produce satisfactory results. Knowledge is just as necessary for this method as it is for in-breeding, and it is sometimes pitiful to see a novice breeder line-breeding to some dog whose outstanding faults have already been obvious in many of his progeny, and who is perhaps closely related to the bitch to which he is to be mated. Exactly the same qualities are needed for line-breeding as for in-breeding, and the distinction between the two forms is not a hard and fast one. The outstanding animal is the first requirement of both.

Out-breeding

This is the opposite of in-breeding, and may be defined as the mating of individuals less closely related than the average.

Genetically it tends to increase heterozygosity and so diminishes prepotency. It is, however, the only way in which new genes can be introduced into a closely in-bred strain. By outcrossing a breeder can combine in his own stock genes from two distinct lines. If the parents have been well selected, the resulting F.1 genotype will be good. It may, however, be a combination of good and bad. But Mendelian segregation will tend to break up the genotype in F.2, and later generations, giving an opportunity of selecting the good and discarding the bad. It is essential to secure the desired genotype at the first cross.

The general result of out-breeding can be summed up as 'to increase individual excellence and diminish breeding worth'. So marked is the individual excellence which may be achieved by the out-bred animal that it has been given a special label, Hybrid Vigour, or Heterosis.

This is well recognized, and one has only to think of the mule as being a good example of hybrid vigour, though hybrid as describing the mule is not quite the same as the genetic hybrid.

Hybrid vigour is most in evidence in the F.1 generation, resulting directly from the cross, and in cases where the parents have possessed different desirable genes, for example when they come from different in-bred lines. It is associated with heterozygosis and the fact that, on the whole, desirable genes are more likely to be dominant than not.

Its precise genetic explanation, as that of its converse, the deterioration sometimes met within in-bred stock, is still gentically uncertain.

Apart from the definite place which an occasional out-cross must have in any in-breeding plan, its main usefulness in dog breeding seems to be to the breeder whose chief concern is with the show-ring. He may easily get a lucky winner. Out-breeding is in fact short-term policy, in-breeding one of long-term.

In connection with out-breeding certain terms are much used and should be defined.

Cross-breeding.　　The mating of two pure-bred animals of different breeds.

Out-crossing.　　Almost synonymous with out-breeding, but should be reserved, strictly speaking, for such a step carried out during a plan of in-breeding, and should carry the implication that the latter is to be resumed directly the out-cross has been made.

Neither in-breeding nor line-breeding is able to produce

any gene not existing in the animals used, and undesirable genes are as likely to be inherited as desirable, as every breeder who uses the methods knows. Provision of new genes or the prevention of fixation of some defect in any in-bred strain, calls for a judicious out-cross.

Every care must be taken to ensure as far as possible that other undesirable genes are not introduced at the same time. A return to in-breeding should be made after the out-cross.

Back-cross.   This has already been described in an earlier chapter. It denotes the mating back of a hybrid, a heterozygote, (or possible hybrid, remembering that the recessive gene is obscured by dominance), to one or other of its homozygous parents. The confusion arises because the term is sometimes restricted to that particular form of back-cross in which a suspected heterozygote is mated back to the recessive homozygous parent (*see* Chapter Ten) for the purpose of assessing phenotype in the resulting generation. The term Test Mating should be employed for this type of back-cross.

ADDENDUM
Vaccination and Duration of Immunity

Vaccination

Protection against distemper, contagious hepatitis, leptospirosis and canine parvo-virus disease can be given in a complete vaccination course, which usually involves two injections. The first injection can be given in some cases, as early as six weeks, but the second injection should not be administered until the puppies are twelve weeks old or over. This recommendation is based on the fact that, before twelve weeks of age, many puppies carry a level of transferred maternal antibodies of distemper and hepatitis which may prevent active immunisation as a result of the inoculation taking place. Today there are many brands and combinations of vaccines available; the best person to advise in a particular situation is your local veterinary surgeon, who is aware of the prevailing local conditions which often can alter one's approach to a vaccin-ation programme.

Duration of Immunity

With the advent of combined vaccines, it is gradually becoming routine to boost a dog's immunity against distemper, hepatitis, leptospiral disease and canine parvo-virus disease with a single combined inoculation every year. Again, the advice of the local veterinary surgeon should be followed since conditions vary from area to area. The duration of immunity also varies according to whether a killed or attenuated-living vaccine is used as can occur with hepatitis vaccination.

The choice of brands and types of vaccine used should very much be the preroga-tive of the veterinary surgeon, rather than the breeder, since many separate factors will influence this choice, not least of which will be the prevalence of infection in the area. Recent work has shown that as the incidence of naturally occurring disease drops with the widespread use of vaccination, so the need for regular boosting becomes more apparent since animals do not get a natural boost from contact with the natural disease as once used to be the case. It cannot be over-emphasized, however, that unvaccinated puppies should, as far as possible, be isolated until their vaccination programme is completed and they have a good workable immunity.

GLOSSARY

ALLELOMORPH, ALLELE (synonymous). One of a pair of genes situated on homologous chromosomes, inherited alternatively with its fellow. The pair usually control con-trasted characters.

Multiple Alleles: a series of genes responsible for gradations of a certain character, occupying the same position (or locus) on a chromosome. Any one individual can carry only two members of such a series.

AUTOSOME, AUTOSOMAL CHROMOSOME. The ordinary body chromosome other than the sex chromosome.

BACK-CROSS. Mating of a hybrid back to one of its parents.

CELL. The unit of living tissue.

CHARACTER. Observable or demonstrable property of an individual due to genetic similarities or differences.

CHROMATID. Half-chromosome, the result of the splitting of each chromosome.

CHROMATIN. The deeply staining network which pervades the cell nucleus and gives rise to chromosomes early in the process of cell division.

CHROMOSOME. Gene-carrying body, arising from the chromatin of a dividing cell.

CROSSING-OVER. The exchange of material together with a block of genes between chromatids during meiosis.

CYTOLOGY. The science of the cell.

CYTOPLASM. Cell protoplasm, other than that of the nucleus.

DOMINANCE. The power of one of a pair of genes to mask the effect of the other member of the pair.

EMBRYO. An organism in the early pre-natal stage of its development.

ENZYMES. Chemical substances which can produce reactions in other substances without themselves undergoing any change. They are called catalysts.

EPISTASIS. The masking of the effect of one gene by another which is not the second member of the pair. A kind of non-allelic dominance.

GAMETE. The germ, or reproductive cells. Sperms in the male; ova, or eggs, in the female.

GENE. Unit of inheritance. Genes are arranged in linear fashion along the chromosomes.

Complementary genes act together to produce an effect different from that of either acting separately.

Modifying Genes alter the action of other (major) genes.

Suppressive Genes act solely to suppress the action of other genes.

GENOTYPE. The constitution of an individual as determined by its total gene content: the hereditary pattern.

GONAD. Sex gland. Ovary (female). Testis (male).

HETEROZYGOUS. Inheriting a given factor from one parent, and its opposite (or allelemorph) from the other.

HOMOLOGOUS. Of the same nature. Of common descent.

HOMOZYGOUS. Inheriting a given factor from both parents.

HORMONE. Internal secretion of endocrine (or ductless) gland. Stimulates the physiological action of other organs.

HYBRID. Heterozygous. Heterozygote. q. v.

HYPOSTASIS. Converse of epistasis. A hypostatic gene is one masked by the action of another which is not its allele, a kind of non-allelic recessive.

LETHAL. Causing death at an early stage of development.

Semi-lethal causing severe disabilities at the same stage.

LINKAGE. Transmission *en bloc* of genes occurring on the same chromosome. Crossing-over (q. v.) interferes with this.

Sex-linked genes are those situated on the X chromosome.

LOCUS. The place of a particular gene on its chromosome.

MEIOSIS. Method of division of sex cells, reductive in character.

MITOSIS. Method of division of cells other than sex cells.

Method of growth from a single cell to a complete individual.

MUTATION. Change in gene or chromosome whereby a heritable variation is brought about.

NUCLEOPLASM. Protoplasm within the nucleus.

NUCLEUS. Most important part of a cell, which controls its various activities.

OVARY. Female sex gland or gonad.

PATHOGENIC. Disease producing.

PHENOTYPE. Visible manifestation, due to the action of environment on the hereditary pattern.

PROTOPLASM. The basis of living matter.

PURE-BREEDING. Having inherited a similar gene in respect of any character from both parents.

RECESSIVE. Opposite of dominant; a gene which is masked by the dominant member of a pair.

RECOMBINATION. A type of variation due to rearrangement of genes.

SEGREGATION (Mendelian). The separation at meiosis of chromosomes and genes.

SIB(S). Progeny of the same parents, irrespective of sex.

SOMATIC. Pertaining to the body, apart from sex cells.

SPERM. Male sex cell or gamete.

TESTIS, TESTICLE. Male sex gland or gonad.

TEST-MATING. Mating of a hybrid (heterozygote) back to a recessive.

VARIATION. Differences between individuals due to
  1. Differences in the hereditary pattern of their cells (genotype). Example: eye colour. These are inherited.
  2. Differences between individuals owing to the action of environment on genotype. Example: docked tails. These are not inherited.

ZYGOTE. The primordial cell, formed by the union of two gametes, male and female.

BIBLIOGRAPHY

Burns, Marca. *The Genetics of the Dog*. Commonwealth Agricultural Bureau 1952.

Burns, Marca and Fraser, Margaret. *Genetics of the Dog*. Oliver & Boyd. 2nd edition 1966.

Darlington and Mather. *The Elements of Genetics*. Allen and Unwin 1949.

Ford, E. M. *Genetics for Medical Students*. Methuen 1942.

Frankling, Eleanor. *The Dalmatian*. Popular Dogs Publishing Co. 4th edition 1974.

George, Wilma. *Elementary Genetics*. Macmillan 1956.

Grüneberg, Hans. *Animal Genetics and Medicine*. Hamish Hamilton Medical Books 1947.

Hagedoorn, A. L. *Animal Breeding*. Crosby Lockwood and Son 1946.

Kalmus, H. *Genetics*. Pelican Press 1948 (new edition 1964).

Little, Clarence C. *The Inheritance of Coat Colour in Dogs*. Comstock Publishing Associates, Cornell University Press 1957.

Robinson, Roy. *Genetics for Dog Breeders*. Pergamon Press 1982.

Sinnott and Dunn. *The Principles of Genetics*. McGraw Hill Book Co. 1939.

Winchester, A. M. *Genetics*. Houghton Mifflin Co., Boston. 2nd edition 1958.

Winge, Ojvind. *Inheritance in Dogs*. Comstock Publishing Co. 1950.

INDEX